Are You Having Fun Yet?

How to Bring the Art of Play Into Your Recovery

Carmen Renee Berry

Thomas Nelson Publishers
Nashville

Copyright © 1992 by Carmen Renee Berry

Published in Nashville, Tennessee, by Thomas Nelson, Inc., and distributed in Canada by Lawson Falle, Ltd., Cambridge, Ontario.

Library of Congress Cataloging-in-Publication Data

Berry, Carmen Renee.
    Are you having fun yet? : how to bring the art of play into your recovery / Carmen Renee Berry.
        p.   cm.
    Includes bibliographical references.
    ISBN 0-8407-3432-8 (pbk.)
    1. Twelve-step programs—Religious aspects—Christianity.
2. Christian life—1960–   I. Title.
BV4596.T88B47   1992
248.8′6—dc20   92-22982
                                                                          CIP

Printed in the United States of America

1 2 3 4 5 6 7 — 97 96 95 94 93 92

to Gail Walker
for her unselfish generosity,
unwavering love and
quirky sense of humor

Acknowledgments

It is with sincerest gratitude that I acknowledge the invaluable contribution of my various "research assistants," who, with no thought of personal hardship or cost to themselves, joined me in a variety of experiences, without which this book would have no illustrations whatsoever . . . and I wouldn't have had any fun either.

I am deeply indebted to:

Joel Miller for decades of laughter and quarterly jaunts to Santa Barbara for spiritual retreat and exploring trendy book stores;

Patricia Luehrs for sharing adventures in snorkeling, exploring the wonders of the zoo, and taking me to the strangest foreign films I've ever seen;

Bobette Buster for introducing me to mud baths and aromatherapy, inviting me to weekend excursions to exotic locations, and entertaining me with bizarre tales from Hollywood;

Bob Parsons and Cathy Smith, my co-creators of the annual Pumpkin Pie Party, for "hanging out" with me every Wednesday night to do crossword puzzles and watch "Doogie Howser, M.D.";

Rene Chansler for our afternoon getaways, munching on nachos and guacamole, and sharing my love for comedy movie matinees;

Rick Fraser for sharing late-morning brunches of chocolate chip waffles and dancing under the stars at the jazz festival;

Stephen Smith for the historic and spontaneous "I just missed my plane so why don't we go to Knott's Berry Farm" adventure;

Suzanne Lake for our annual English High Tea and, with her husband, Kevin, for throwing the best Christmas parties Joel and I have ever attended;

Daniel Psaute who writes me outrageous letters, shares with me his love for George MacDonald, and regularly flies into my life for a week of lively chatter, two or three movies a day, and great one-liners;

Vanessa Carlisle, who always makes me laugh, for sharing with me a love of collecting movie scripts and a smile that has turned many a dark day into hope;

Erica Carlisle for introducing me to TGIFridays and for afternoons of creating delicious delights for English High Tea;

Cynthia Morgan, with whom I share priceless childhood memories, for the many nights we sang and played our guitars, the youthful dreams we entrusted to each other, and the friendship that has endured through all the changes in our lives;

Joe and Sheila Palacios for sharing with me their enthusiasm for life and passion for making pumpkin pie goo;

Mark Baker for years of support and an unforgettable evening riding a Harley Davidson to the Hollywood Bowl;

Ron and Cathi Salsbury, who provided me with a sane and safe place in those desperate days early in my recovery, for sharing my tears of sadness and unrestrained laughter;

Irene Flores for hours of invaluable advice on how to deal with men and for dragging me out onto the slopes so I'd take my first skiing lesson;

Jim Kermath who, as my "play hero," inspired me to continue skiing, got me to watch an entire basketball game on TV, and helped give my inner child a safe place to come out and play;

The Kitzmiller Clan—John, Joel, and Chris—for one of the funnest days I've had on the slopes and who, inadvertently, took me down my first black diamond run;

Manny Ocampo for his immortal words, "Toil 'neath the sun should be matched in equal measure with tokens of whimsy";

The slightly off-center gang at Recovery Partnership for making work a fun place to be—Dale and Juanita Ryan, Betsy Reed, Pat and Marsha Means, Robin C. Wainwright, Don McIntosh, Phil Leidy, and Linda Kondracki;

Calvin Slater, my highly respectable attorney, who introduced me to the delights of Indian food, the finer aspects of belly dancing, and how to wear three birthday hats on your head at the same time, in public, and not lose your sense of style;

My bodywork support group, Susan Latta, Kate O'Sullivan, and Virginia Frederich, for hours of laughter over turkey sandwiches and a lifetime supply of tortilla chips;

Robert Myers for inviting me to a Bible study and taking me swimming at Raging Waters instead;

Yang Shim Chang whose support gives me hope and whose insight gives me clarity when I need it most;

Bill Skinner, the funniest man I've ever met, for reconnecting me with my youth and for sending me strange greeting cards and who keeps promising to take me rafting on the Sacramento River (hint, hint);

Bill Rich who taught me how to waltz and, along with Bill Skinner and parrot, Delilah, for a brief moment one Sunday morning, formed the greatest gospel quartet this world has ever known;

Joanne Feldmeth who has supported me through the process of writing via pep talks on my answering machine and afternoon coffee breaks at Green Street Restaurant;

Friends who have shared Glen Ivy Hot Springs getaways, such as Connie Lillas, Coleen Friend, and Toni Johnson;

George Eckart and Frank Azzarriti for their enthusiasm for fun, our memorable day in Laguna, and nights out on the dance floor;

Craig McNair Wilson for sharing my love for stand-up comedy and witty banter and for letting me wear his leather jacket;

Charles Swan, whose kindness, sensitivity, and body work expertise have helped me release my fear, sadness, and anger and more deeply enjoy life;

The Nice to be Kneaded folks whose massage and saunas have rejuvenated my soul—Martin Nunez, Laura Nunez, Timothy Bennett, Blanca O'Neal, Cheryl Hewitt, Martti Makinen, and Rosa Sanchez;

Impact Personal Safety, especially the instructors in Santa Monica, for teaching me how to fight back and regain my sense of personal power;

Paul Roberts, my therapist, who has not only made it safe for me to cry but also safe for me to laugh.

In taking these various adventures and turning them into a manuscript, I owe my deepest gratitude to Roy M. Carlisle, my agent, editor, confidant, and friend. Roy's talent as an editor is unmatched and his ability to put up with my "artistic temperament" has saved many a chapter from the trash can. As many of his other authors have said, I can't imagine writing a book without him.

I want to express a special thanks to Noreen Naughton, Ann Chamberlin, Joann Connors, and Pauline Krismanich of Immaculate Heart Community for providing me with a haven in which to work on this manuscript.

And to all the folks at Thomas Nelson under the able leadership of Bruce Barbour for showing me what a joy it is to experience a publishing house working as a team on behalf of writers and readers;

My warmest appreciation to Ron Haynes, acquisitions editor, who saw potential in this project and provided me with kind support throughout the process;

Jane Jones who deserves applause for transforming the manuscript into its final form;

Lori Quinn and Amy Clark for their patient coordination of the final delightful dustjacket;

Louetta Sayne for her patience with numerous faxes and her graciousness throughout the ups and downs of contracting, writing, editing, and publishing.

Contents

1

Rekindle Your Hope in the Possibility of Play

Surveying the faces of the other group members in the room, I suspected that they weren't having any more success than I at making the hard metal chairs feel comfortable. Nevertheless, I shifted my weight for the umpteenth time and focused my attention once again on Cindy, the young woman who was sharing.

Her knuckles were white as she strangled the sides of her chair. "I am so discouraged," she confessed sadly. "I've been sober for five months. It's been hard, as you all know." She paused, looking up at the nodding heads around her, mine included. I remembered Cindy's five months of sobriety and the two not-so-sober months before. It had been hard for her to relinquish her dependency on alcohol, but for five months, Cindy had lived a sober life.

Cindy continued, "There were nights I didn't think I could go another minute without a drink. But I kept telling myself, 'Hang in there, it will be worth it.'" She stopped as silent tears began to flow down her face. I squirmed again, in yet another futile effort to make peace with my chair.

After a long silence, she continued. "What am I doing wrong? If I'm sober, why am I miserable? If I'm better, then why don't I *feel* better?" Leaning forward, Cindy looked each of us in the eye, as if we all knew the secret but were willfully keeping it from her. "Maybe I'm missing the point somehow, but do any of you have any fun? I'm not drinking, but so what? When do I start feeling happy? How do I fill this gnawing emptiness? I mean, what's the payoff?"

Her questions hung over the group like a suffocating blanket. I squirmed again, only this time more than the chair was making me feel uncomfortable.

As I listened to Cindy express her despair, I began asking myself similar questions. If addiction is painful and recovery is painful, why choose recovery over addiction? Why uncover the horrible childhood memories our brains have tried to forget? Why embrace the pain of reality when, at least for a time, the hurt could be numbed through alcohol, food, sex, work, relationships, or flat-out denial? As Cindy asked all of us in group that night, what *is* the payoff? Is recovery just one painful experience after another, or is there a time when it all becomes easier? How do we get what we need? Is it possible to enjoy life again?

For a Good Time, Call . . . Anyone Who Is Not in Recovery

Wherever I go as a workshop and seminar presenter, and in my own recovery and personal life as well, I meet a bevy of courageous people, each valiantly in the process of overcoming some life-threatening addiction, childhood trauma, or life-changing challenge. As I listen to their stories, often with tears in my eyes, words like *awe-inspiring, intensely dedicated, inspirational, tenacious,* and *brave* come to mind. Their commitment to recovery serves to bolster my own courage in facing the often difficult journey of healing and growth. Rarely, however, do I meet someone who is having a good time.

Let's be honest. The recovery movement is not known for its upbeat flavor or its happy-go-lucky promises. Recovery is, after all, a matter of life and death. I remember, in 1985, waking up in the middle of the night screaming, terrified with the knowledge that I was breaking, emotionally and physically, under the crushing weight of my addiction. As a codependent, I carried an unrealistic burden to "save" the world, which drove me into an eighteen-hour-a-day, seven-day work week. Feeling too guilty to rest and too ashamed to ask for help, my life became a swirling hurricane of activity, until one day, I collapsed.

All of the people I've met who consider themselves to be "in recovery" can tell a similar story of "hitting bottom." There's Denny who describes waking up in a filthy hotel room after a three-day drunk with no memory and no self-respect. Jane, now slim and fit, is still under a doctor's care for a heart condition aggravated by the excessive weight she once carried due to her addiction to food. As a former pastor, now rebuilding his life, John's eyes still tear as he describes the day his wife left him once she found out about his sexual addiction to prostitutes. Mary carries scars on her wrists from the night she tried to put an end to the childhood memories of her father's sexual assaults. Candy still trembles when she recalls waking up in the emergency room, tubes flowing from her body, as the hospital team fought to save her from another drug overdose.

None of us went into recovery because it was fun. With our denial shattered, we were backed into a corner and confronted with a choice—honesty or insanity, recovery or death. At that moment in my life, the pain was so unbearable and my defeat so undeniable, I was finally willing to cry out for help. Without knowing it at the time, I was taking the first of the Twelve Steps. I admitted I was powerless over my addiction. My life had become unmanageable.

Like many others, I began my recovery journey with tears in my eyes and a fragile hope that my life could be restored to sanity by a Power greater than my own. I wish I could report that since I began my recovery in 1985 life has been one enjoyable adventure after another. But I can't. Facing the truth about certain childhood experiences, taking moral inventories, and making amends for the damage I have caused has been painful. All too often, recovery points somberly toward sobriety and promises us hard work, tearful confrontations, a lifetime of attending Twelve Step meetings, and healing somewhere off in the future.

In fact, some branches of the movement claim we can never relax, confident in our recovery, since, regardless of the duration of our sobriety, we will always be addicts. As addicts in recovery, so the claim goes, we will always be one drink away, one sexual encounter away, or one chocolate chip cookie away from plunging headlong, out of control, back into the depths of our compulsions. Living on the brink of chaos, fearful of a life-threatening relapse, can certainly take the fun out of life.

Soberly sober, many have attained sobriety over their particular addiction, only to find their lives disappointingly stark. In spite of consistently working the Twelve Steps and regularly attending their support groups, a motivating passion for living seems elusive.

Others, once victims of childhood abuse and neglect, may now consider themselves survivors. But life has become simply that—merely a struggle for survival. As once-forgotten painful memories continue to erupt into consciousness, recovery for a child abuse survivor can seem to promise only endless encounters with grief.

Some, facing unavoidable life-altering situations, such as the death of a loved one, divorce, major physical illness, midlife crisis, burnout, or unemployment, sift among the pieces of their lives searching for something familiar or Someone who can help. Usually disoriented and often frightened, those in life transitions may feel grateful just to have something solid to cling to, viewing fun and enjoyment as luxuries long past or fantasies far off in the future.

Are You Having Fun Yet?

To see if you may be immersing yourself in the pain, the losses, and the dark side of life while pleasure, laughter, and light-hearted fun elude you, ask yourself the following questions.

- Have you lost faith that you can have all of your needs met?
- Does your life lack spontaneity and a childlike enjoyment of each day?
- Do you feel uncomfortable or even guilty at times when you receive attention from others?
- Do you often feel deprived of what you need?
- Are you regularly disappointed by the consideration you receive from friends and family?
- Have you felt dissatisfied with your life, but unclear as to what would make you happy?
- Even though you may believe in God or a Higher Power, do you secretly doubt you are loved?
- Are you concerned that if you address your own needs, you may take more than your share and appear selfish?
- Do you see experiences, such as rest, vacations, sports activities, or parties, as luxuries?
- Do you put effort into "cutting back" on enjoyable experiences as a regular way to manage your finances?
- Do you suspect that you unconsciously sabotage your chances for happiness?
- If you do take a vacation, host a party, or participate in potentially enjoyable experiences, do you often find yourself disappointed at the outcome?
- Would you prefer to go without something you need or want rather than ask someone for assistance, thereby risking rejection?
- Have you given up hope that anyone could love you?
- Do you routinely feel that you give more to others than they give back to you?

At times in my life, I have been able to answer yes to all of these questions. In fact, it wasn't until the fifth year of my recovery that it even occurred to me I could enjoy life, here and now.

A few people, far too few unfortunately, have discovered how to recover, not only their sobriety, but also their passion for life. Along their journey, they have incorporated the thoughts and techniques, the beliefs and skills, that equip them, not only to face their pain and grieve their losses, but also to celebrate their successes and enjoy the journey. Sorting through the rubble of their lives, they have not only picked up the parts of themselves labeled "brave" and "committed," but also "playful," "mischievous," and "contented."

Incorporating the capacity to play into one's recovery is an art that can easily be overlooked. While recovery certainly has serious ramifications, we may fall prey to taking ourselves far too seriously and deprive ourselves of one of life's most valuable opportunities—the chance to enjoy ourselves and each other.

Pursue a New Paradigm of Play

When I was a little girl, the neighborhood children and I used to play a rather elaborate game we called "treasure hunt." One of us would be the "Pirate," and would hide a treasure, usually some candy or snack, somewhere in the neighborhood, while the rest of us waited inside one of our homes. The Pirate would draw a map of the chosen area and would also hide clues that would eventually lead us to the buried treasure. Most of the time, this was a great game and we enjoyed it immensely.

One afternoon, however, Chuckie was the Pirate. Now, Chuckie was a nice kid and we all liked him, but he had a horrible sense of direction. The map he drew for us in no way correlated with the reality of our neighborhood. Consequently we roamed from house to house for over an hour, becoming more and more frustrated. Chuckie was so distressed that he forgot where he had hidden the clues. Finally in desperation, he simply led us to the tree under which he had hidden our snacks. Once munching on our candy, we decided we would forgive Chuckie, but would never let him be Pirate on his own again. He would always need to have one of his crew help him draw the map.

Our ability to find our way through life and get what we want and need is based, in part, on the reliability of the maps we use. If the maps are up to date and reflect the terrain, we are able to make our way. But if you have a map similar to the one Chuckie drew that summer day so many years ago, the journey can be frustrating, disappointing, and disorienting.

As M. Scott Peck clearly describes in *The Road Less Traveled*, "our view of reality is like a map with which to negotiate the terrain of life. If the map is true and accurate, we will generally know where we are, and if we have decided where we want to go, we will generally know how to get there. If the map is false and inaccurate, we generally will be lost."[1]

I feel it is safe to say that if we in this society are anything, we are lost. Change occurs so rapidly and erratically that many of the explanations that served our parents are utterly useless to us now.

Incorporating play into our recovery journeys may require a "paradigm shift." As Stephen Covey points out in *The Seven Habits of Highly Effective People*, a paradigm is "commonly used today to mean a model, theory, perception, assumption, or frame of reference. In the more general sense, it's the way we 'see' the world—not in terms of our visual sense of sight, but in terms of perceiving, understanding, interpreting."[2]

Each of us operates out of our own personal view of reality, a paradigm we initially acquire through influences and experiences in childhood. Most people take their personal paradigm for granted. Some may not even be aware that they hold a particular perspective, one that could be questioned or altered. In fact, unless a person takes the time and energy to identify his or her personal paradigm, this perspective is generally held unconsciously and acted upon without question.

Any afternoon turn the television dial to the various talk shows, and you'll be bombarded with differing, if not conflicting, paradigms of reality. Competition runs high among paradigm promoters, whether they are religiously based, psychologically grounded, or, in the case of this book, rooted in a paradigm of recovery.

Thomas Kuhn originally coined the phrase "paradigm shift" to describe the process by which a society or an individual discards one map of reality for another. In his book *The Structure of Scientific Revolutions* he explains that "paradigms gain their status because they are more successful than their competitors in solving a few problems."[3] Since reality is so complex, however, we have yet to devise a paradigm that solves *all* of the problems. What we are all faced with, then, is a continual process of revising, rejecting, reworking, reviewing, and replacing our current paradigms with ones that may answer the questions just a little more satisfactorily.

While this process may be difficult, anxiety producing, and confusing at times, the capacity to revise your personal paradigm is the cornerstone of mental health. In order to progress from infancy to healthy adulthood, we are continually confronted with the need to revise our maps of reality. Those who, as children, learned to be flexible, creative, and discerning, are able to navigate these turbulent waters with minimal duress. Most of us, however, having clung to distorted views of reality, are fearful of failure and unskilled at negotiating change.

Rekindle Your Hope in the Possibility of Play

As Peck adeptly points out, the "process of active clinging to an outmoded view of reality is the basis for much mental illness."[4] When we were children, we were, in fact, significantly less powerful and adept than we are today as adults. Yet many of us unconsciously cling to a personal paradigm that continues to render us helpless, even though we are no longer dependent upon our parents for survival. No matter how miserable our childhoods may have been, I believe we can discard our outdated personal paradigms and replace them with maps that promote a joyous adulthood, with ample time for rest, intimacy, and fun.

We all crave to be loved and nurtured, to play and enjoy our lives. Regardless of the tenacity of addictions, the extent of childhood abuse, or the impact of life-changing experiences, we all long to laugh and to play. The first step in incorporating the art of play into your recovery is embracing a new personal paradigm, one that insists it is possible to enjoy life.

If you answered yes to several of the questions on page 5, you quite possibly have relinquished your right to play by holding on to a paradigm that says "it's too late" or "no one cares" or "good things just don't happen to me." As a result, you are missing the chance to enjoy life to its fullest potential. In the following chapters, we will take one step at a time toward rebuilding hope in the possibility of play, relearning the skills needed to play, and sharing with others our passion for living.

2

Embrace the Perspective of Abundance

In my seminars I ask participants, "What is lacking in your life?" One participant will call out, "I don't have enough time!" and another will insist "Put money on that list." As the overhead projector beams the list on the screen, the transparency quickly fills as I list their areas of need, such as energy, support, understanding, rest, time for spiritual reflection, love, sleep, peace, fun. I've never worked with a group that had trouble identifying an abundance of things of which they didn't have enough!

Next, I ask the participants to identify areas in which they experience abundance. "Work!" someone usually calls out. "I've got plenty of stress!" confesses another. So entrenched are we in the Perspective of Scarcity that, even when trying to identify areas in which we have our needs met, it is easier to find areas of "abundant" need!

I usually reframe these suggestions as "a lack of leisure time" and "inadequate nurturance" and urge the group to identify positive areas of abundance. Usually silence is the response. One person may say, "I have enough friends." Another says, "I feel close to God, so I feel enough spiritual support." The lists of "Areas of Abundance" are usually quite short. One group I worked with couldn't identify even one area in which they felt they had enough of what they wanted or needed in life.

Usually someone in the group will ask, "But is it really possible to have our needs met? What is the use of identifying these areas of need if we are powerless to get what we want?"

These are legitimate questions. What if you were able to get all of your needs met? If there were enough for you, would there be enough left over for me? If I go after what I want, doesn't it mean that I'll have to walk over someone else or deprive others of what they need? How could there be enough for all of us?

Passive Dependency

We all have legitimate needs. Some needs are physical, such as food, safety, exercise, sleep, and sexual expression. We all have emotional needs, such as acceptance, attention, and love. As spiritual beings, each of us needs a sense of purpose and a meaningful connection to God. And as we exercise our mental capacities, we have a need for intellectual stimulation, valid information, a reliable understanding of our world, and personal guidance.

It is really quite simple—when we have our needs met, we are free to enjoy our lives. When we are deprived of what we need, we experience pain and are unable to embrace healthy joy or love others creatively.

This is especially true if our legitimate needs were not met when we were children. All children have legitimate dependency needs, which must be met to grow into healthy adulthood. As a result of receiving insufficient childhood nurture and security, many of us still feel powerless to get our needs met. We take into adulthood a passive stance toward the meeting of our own legitimate dependency needs. Instead of feeling competent to address our legitimate needs, we often experience an intense longing and neediness. As a consequence, we may develop "passive dependent personalities."

I was first confronted with my own passive dependency several years back while reading M. Scott Peck's book, *The Road Less Traveled*. Peck describes passive dependent adults as those who did not receive adequate "affection, attention and care during their childhood." Peck explains that these children grow into adults with "an inner sense of insecurity, a feeling of 'I don't have enough' and a sense that the world is unpredictable and ungiving. . . . As a matter of fact, it is no accident that the most common disturbance that passive dependent people manifest beyond their relationships to others is dependency on drugs and alcohol. Theirs is the 'addictive personality.'"[1]

It was a shock for me to read these words, for they rang true in the deepest parts of my soul. I had worked hard to hide my passivity and powerlessness regarding my own life by creating a facade of excessive activity and competence for helping others. No effort was too great in hiding my own feelings of dependency. No, I was too frightened to acknowledge my neediness. Instead, I carefully constructed an exterior of rigid independence. But when my "active independent" mask cracked, I was confronted with my passive dependency.

Children do not have the same power of choice that adults have. As children, we are dependent upon our parents for our survival. But as adults, this is no longer true. We can provide for ourselves. However, if we have yet to experience the genuine satisfaction of our legitimate childhood needs for dependency, it doesn't matter how old we are. We still need to have those needs met. We cannot move beyond this stage until our legitimate needs for dependency are addressed.

Scarcity vs. Abundance

Consider these facts:

- Each day thousands of people die of starvation on this planet.

- As we enter the 1990s unemployment is rampant. Everywhere we look, the homeless fill our streets. Recent statistics claim that there are anywhere from 400,000 to 3,000,000 homeless people in the United States, 10 percent of them families with children.
- Suicides are on the rise, especially among teenagers. In 1990, there were 30,780 reported cases of suicide in this country, and 5,000 of those were under the age of eighteen.
- Divorce continues to be a plaguing social problem. In 1990 there were 1,170,000 divorces compared to 2,436,000 marriages in the United States. That is a shocking 48% rate of marital failure, even with the news about supposed declining divorce rates due to AIDS, the resurgence of the family, and tough economic times keeping people together.

Why are these people starving to death? Is it because there isn't enough food? Why is poverty spreading in this country? Is there a shortage of wealth on the planet? Why are people killing themselves? Is there a shortage of hope? Why are so many marriages failing? Have we run out of love?

In fact, ample food is produced on this planet, more than enough for every person to be properly fed. These men, women, and children are dying horrible deaths, not because of a scarcity of food, but because they are caught in dysfunctional political systems that operate out of a Perspective of Scarcity.

Are unemployment and poverty on the rise because there is suddenly a scarcity of money on the planet? No. There is sufficient wealth available, but it is being controlled by a shrinking number of people who are engaged in economic systems that foster excess for a few and scarcity for the majority.

There is enough hope on this planet for all of us to live vital lives and enough love for every marriage to succeed. So why are people giving up hope and killing themselves or abandoning their marriages? We are caught in a global illusion that there just isn't enough—not enough love, not enough self-esteem, not enough safety, not enough money, not enough happiness, or not enough hope—for us all to be healthy and live in peace.

I believe that the experience of scarcity, an experience so common in our world, is a result of not receiving the proper nurture and protection needed as children. Having developed a passive dependent stance in life, a large portion of the population feels powerless to get their legitimate needs met. This sense of powerlessness is passed on to others. If we embrace a Perspective of Scarcity, we will naturally hoard what little we have, thereby depriving others of what we could share. Instead of nurturing each other, we have become a competitive world, competing for nurturance, attention, and love, convinced there's a limited supply of these necessary items.

The Perspective of Scarcity is rampant in our society, propagated by the media, by many religious systems, and, sometimes, even by our own families. Many of us live as if we are on a life raft with insufficient rations to survive. We eye each other, wondering who will be the next to die or who should volunteer to give up their small portion to save the others. Those of us who consider ourselves codependents believe this lie to our core. We continually give up our own portion for others because we are sure that there isn't enough for everyone. The Perspective of Scarcity is accepted as a fact of life. The only choices before us, as addicts, is who will go without and how can we numb the pain.

Succumbing to the Perspective of Scarcity

Melody

Melody angrily tugged at her sweater, trying to hide her thighs as she rode the bus toward her mother's apartment. "I hate these family dinners," she grumbled to herself. "I can hear it now: 'Oh, Mel, dear, haven't you even tried to keep to your diet?'" She grimaced as she caught her large reflection in the bus window. "Why can't I lose weight? Why am I so fat and ugly? And, why do I keep going over to my mother's and letting her hassle me this way?" Her image blurred as tears filled her eyes.

She thought to herself, "I can hear my mother now: 'I'll tell you what the problem is, Melody. You have such a nice face but you have no discipline. You are just like your father, he always ate like a horse. If you weren't so lazy and would exercise . . .'"

Melody sighed in deep sorrow. "Maybe she's right. I can't do it. I'll be fat all my life. Why even try?"

Jack

Jack re-opened the bank statement as if looking at it one more time would magically make the numbers change. "I can't believe it. Where did the money go?" He sat in the car, not wanting to go into the house and let Marilyn see the statement. "Why can't I get ahead financially? I really thought this last project would pay off. Why can't I pick a winner?" He laid his head against the steering wheel. "Why can't I be more like my brother? Everything he does turns to gold. But not for me. Why am I such a flop? No wonder Marilyn is ashamed of me. Why would a woman like her want to be married to a failure like me?"

Allison

Allison dabbed at her puffy, red eyes, futilely trying to camouflage hours of crying with eye shadow and mascara. "There," she thought, "that's not so bad." But as she turned from the mirror she caught sight of the letter she'd just received from Randy. With renewed anguish, the tears flowed unchecked, streaking her makeup down her cheeks. "How can I ever live without him? Why did he leave me? What did I do to mess this up? Why did I act like such an idiot last night?" She couldn't stop the dark thoughts or the blaming questions. Throwing herself on the bed in defeat she sobbed. "Who could ever love me? What meaning can life have for me without Randy?"

Melody, Jack, and Allison have a couple of things in common. First, they are all, to one degree or another, experiencing a challenge, a crisis. From time to time, all of us are confronted with disappointment, rejection, loss, and mistakes in judgment. None of us is perfect, nor do we have control over a wide variety of things that happen to us in our lives.

The second thing Melody, Jack, and Allison have in common is the way they choose to respond to their challenges. We may not be able to control everything that comes into our lives, but we do have a choice about how we will respond to these events and whether we will operate out of a Perspective of Scarcity or of Abundance. Melody, Jack, and Allison have chosen to respond to their problems out of a Perspective of Scarcity.

How is this revealed? By the types of questions they ask themselves.

- Why am I so fat and ugly?
- Why even try?
- Why can't I get ahead financially?
- Why am I such a flop?
- Why would a woman like her want to be married to a failure like me?
- What did I do to mess this up?
- Why did I act like such an idiot last night?
- Who could ever love me?

The consequences of operating from scarcity are disastrous. When difficult situations arise, situations that occur to *everyone on the planet*, we immediately assume the most negative, self-blaming, defeated posture. We naturally embrace the dark side of life, more able to see loss and death than we are able to see opportunity and resurrection.

We begin with an unconscious assumption that we cannot have what we need. As a consequence, we do not put effort into getting our needs met. Instead, we focus all our creativity on justifying our deprivation or abuse. We come up with ways we can do without what we need. At a moment's notice, we can list a myriad of reasons why we don't deserve what we want.

And what about those around us who are getting what they need and want? We proudly declare those folks to be "selfish," "materialistic," or some other shaming criticism. Convinced we are inferior and deserving of mistreatment, we respond not with outrage at the abuse, but by funneling our anger at ourselves.

Our minds are very obedient. When we ask ourselves questions, our minds will do their best to give us answers. Unfortunately, when we ask ourselves scarcity questions, our minds will obediently respond, *always* coming up with scarcity answers. Look again at these scarcity questions. Study them and see how damaging scarcity questions can be.

When Melody asks herself, "Why am I so fat and ugly?" her brain searches for an answer. Her mind tells her, "Melody, you are so fat and ugly because you are lazy, like your father, undisciplined and hopeless."

When Jack asks scarcity questions, such as "Why can't I get ahead financially?" "Why am I such a flop?" and "Why would a woman like her want to be married to a failure like me?" his brain obediently looks for scarcity answers. He concludes that he is inferior to his brother and undeserving of his marriage.

Worse yet, Jack may even pose these questions to his wife, perhaps hoping for reassurance. But when Jack asks his wife, her brain responds similarly and she will also provide scarcity answers. She may be able to fend off his doubts for awhile, but before long she also will be wondering why she stays with a man who is "inferior" and "undeserving" of her love.

Allison, entrenched in scarcity thinking, can ask only demeaning and shaming questions of herself. "What did I do to mess this up? Why did I act like such an idiot last night? Who could ever love me?" Of course, her mind will obediently try to answer these questions with responses like, "You always say the wrong thing," "Randy is too good for you," "No one will ever want you," and "You'll be alone forever."

Discovering Abundance

Step by step, day by day, my recovery has led me to believe in the Perspective of Abundance. My belief in abundance has grown, like the sprouting of a delicate seed that becomes a great tree, growing slowly and quietly, until it holds strong and firm. As many truths in life, my discovery of the Perspective of Abundance came through a series of paradoxical experiences.

In order to survive beyond my burnout, I realized I had to ask for help by admitting my lack of strength, my lack of understanding, my lack of power. But I loathed asking for help. I valued self-reliance, not humility. I wanted to be independent, not dependent. And yet, through the process of asking for help, and, surprisingly enough, receiving what I needed, I have become more able to take responsibility for my life.

For years I resisted revealing the reality of my past and openly acknowledging the specific ways I was victimized because I feared I'd be left powerless and ashamed. To my surprise, once I acknowledged my victimization, I began to feel the genuine power of my potential and was able to discard the label "Victim." When I ceased pretending that the religious beliefs I had been raised to embrace were sufficient, surprisingly enough, I came face to face with a God who was genuinely available to me. In identifying specific areas of need and acknowledging that my experience of life was one of deprivation and scarcity, I began to enjoy the abundance available. A belief in abundance is rooted in the ability to trust those aspects or persons who are, in fact, trustworthy.

My lessons in "trustworthy trust" included learning to trust my Higher Power. When I began my recovery, I had what I now call "an eye for evil." I was able to see all of the dark and tragic aspects of life, but I was completely blind to the positive ways God may be involved in the world. As a result of this view of life, this Perspective of Scarcity, I lost my faith in a Higher Power that could act on my behalf. My prayer was that my eyes would be opened to whatever good might be in the world and for my heart to be opened to whatever abundance may exist.

Much of what I am sharing here is lessons I have learned as a result of God's responding to my request. I can believe in abundance because now I am able to see the abundance. When I started on this journey, all I could see was the scarcity. Regardless of which belief system a person may adopt, one of scarcity or one of abundance, the belief becomes a self-fulfilling prophecy. A belief in scarcity produces an experience of scarcity. However, a belief in abundance produces an experience of abundance. I found that if I opened myself to the death and resurrection process, I began to experience rebirth, in small ways at first. But if I closed myself off from abundance, scarcity was all that was available to me.

As my eyes grew more accustomed to noticing the nurturance available to me, I accumulated new experiences of trust, abundance, and renewal. I began to learn to trust myself. Avidly, I studied and practiced a variety of techniques used in deciphering the messages given to us through the unconscious, such as dream interpretation, meditation, prayer, active imagination, journaling, painting, and dance. Slowly, but surely, I tested this new knowledge, separating misinterpretations from the truth and the wishes from reliable guidance.

As a child I was taught that we were created in God's image, but I didn't have a sense of what that meant to me personally. While I do not claim to fully understand this spiritual truth, I have come to believe that our unconscious minds were created by God to aid us in our healing and growth. Our unconscious minds naturally push us toward facing the truth. We err, not by giving the unconscious too much power, but in distrusting or misinterpreting its messages.

After years of trial and error, I now know that when I am confused or unclear as to which decision to make, God will provide me with guidance through my unconscious processes. An insight might come through a dream or an image I receive while praying. Sometimes I uncover information through active imagination or through my body work sessions. I regularly receive massage and body work sessions, thereby allowing my body to teach me about myself. Sometimes I understand better what I feel emotionally by becoming more aware of how I am feeling physically. I may be able to deny feeling emotional stress, but I can't deny a huge knot in my shoulder or tightness in my calf muscle.

Body work is especially helpful for those of us adept at numbing ourselves to our true feelings. From it I learn how I carry stress and how best to care for myself. My body has even given me information about what might have happened to me in the past and how I can best protect and nurture myself in the present. Consistently and faithfully, I receive accurate and helpful guidance from myself to myself, knowing that this process is created and directed by a loving God.

Another important lesson of abundance is learning how and when to trust other people. Out of a desperate need for support, I began seeing a therapist. Week after week, my needs were acknowledged. Time after time, he nurtured, instructed, supported, and cared for me. Perhaps most importantly, my therapist believed in me and believed my story. More and more abundance was accumulated into my experience of life as my legitimate dependency needs were met.

In the dark secrets of my past, I had believed one of the many lies of scarcity—that the truth was hard to find. Through therapy, I realized that there is no scarcity of truth. To the contrary, truth is abundant, identifiable, and even acceptable. I now see that while the truth has always been available to me, the dysfunctional belief system I accepted as a child obscured my vision.

In addition to my therapist, my friends and support group also responded to my needs in myriad ways: by engaging in hours of conversation, surprising me with deliveries of flowers, confronting my misconceptions, laughing at my jokes, and sharing a variety of adventures. My eyes opened a little wider to the possibility of nurturance, the possibility that there might actually be enough of what I need, if only I could learn how to receive the nurture.

"Is it possible," I asked myself, "that maybe, just maybe, the deprivation of my past does not have to be the blueprint for my future? Can I possibly relate in a healthier way to those I love and want to love? Can I change self-defeating patterns into success and enjoyment? Is it really possible to have enough of what I need?" To each of these questions, now I can respond with a jubilant Yes! To state this simply, I believe in abundance because I have had repeated experiences in which my legitimate dependency needs have been met.

If There Is Enough, Why Am I Not Getting My Share?

It is fairly easy to see that many of us aren't getting what we need. Many, once acknowledging their deprivation, assume that their experience of scarcity proves that abundance is impossible. Remember this truth—*What we have experienced in the past does not determine what we will be able to enjoy in the future*. Because you are not receiving nurturance at this moment, does not mean that it is unavailable to you.

What we can conclude, however, is that for a variety of possible reasons you are not experiencing abundance at this time. Perhaps the options available are outside your grasp at the moment because your hands are holding a little too tightly to the Perspective of Scarcity.

I believe there are three general stages in recovery: dependence, independence, and interdependence. The tremendous success of the Twelve Steps, can be credited in part to powerfully addressing our feelings of powerlessness. Encouraged to acknowledge our need for a Higher Power and group support, the recovery movement has given many of us a safe place in which to admit that we feel passively dependent.

It is currently in fashion to criticize the recovery movement for its emphasis on dependency by claiming that such tenets cripple the development of individuals, keeping them from becoming autonomous and self-reliant. I do not disagree with these criticisms as much as I believe the critics do not take their argument far enough. Independence is not the goal. We seek interdependence, a healthy intimacy possible only between two independent people who have had their dependency needs satisfied.

None of us can experience a genuine sense of independence until our legitimate dependency needs are met. And none of us can be genuinely intimate with another person until we have clearly defined ourselves as separate beings. Only when we have received attention can we believe that we are important. Only when we accumulate enough hugs to offset childhood abuse can we authentically experience touch as a source of nurture. Only when we are loved are we capable of loving.

The first stage of recovery, honoring legitimate dependency needs, is an absolutely necessary step toward healing and growth. By attending support groups, going to therapy, working the Steps, and participating in other aspects of recovery work, I have been able to acknowledge my legitimate needs for nurturance and safety. But, as many of the critics assert, dependency is not the goal. It is an integral part of the journey.

As I moved into the second stage, independence, the emphasis moved toward taking self-responsibility and exercising individual choice. My attention shifted from looking to others for my nurture to ways I could care for myself. Like a young child taking pride in learning how to tie her own shoes, I take pride in learning how to protect myself from misuse rather than looking to others for protection. I enjoy creating ways to nurture myself, rather than always feeling dependent on someone else's care.

The third stage, interdependency, draws the focus away from ourselves as solitary individuals and toward our abilities to establish mutually beneficial relationships. The skills needed in this stage include negotiation, supporting the growth of others, and creating safe places for all persons involved. Developing "win-win" strategies of enjoyment with those around me becomes an interest, rather than finding that all my attention is wrapped up in my own experience. Creating intimacy through play becomes an important goal.

The following chapters move through these stages, from addressing our legitimate needs for safety and nurture, through identifying what we can do for ourselves, and to creating ways we can enjoy each other.

Only you can assess where you are in this process. If you are experiencing a sense of scarcity, likely many of your legitimate dependency needs have yet to be satisfied. By recognizing the importance of your legitimate needs, you can cooperate with this process, accelerating the healing process.

Many of us may not experience the sense of self-esteem, financial stability, personal safety, or level of intimacy that we want, but that deprivation is not due to a lack of opportunity. The experience of scarcity is rooted in our dysfunctional ways of relating to each other, as individuals, as groups, and as countries. I firmly believe that we all can experience the abundance available, but only as we discard our belief in scarcity and open our eyes to what is realistically possible. In asserting my belief in the Perspective of Abundance, I do not support those who are exploiting the weak, the poor, and the disenfranchised. To the contrary, I call us to a new level of fairness, a compassionate distribution of resources and a realistic hope of mutuality and caring.

Many of us have journeyed into recovery and come to a place of sobriety, yet we haven't discarded our Perspective of Scarcity. We still shame ourselves for feeling needy and powerless to get these needs met. While we are no longer actively abusing ourselves through the misuse of alcohol, drugs, relationships, working, eating, or sex, as long as we retain a Perspective of Scarcity, sobriety is merely another way in which we deprive ourselves. Sobriety becomes another deprivation experience, the deprivation of what little relief from pain our former addictions provided. Only when we discard our Perspective of Scarcity and embrace the Perspective of Abundance does our sobriety become the entry point to living life to its passionate, fulfilling, and exciting potential.

Settle for Nothing Less Than Enough

Transforming our lives into experiences of joy and abundance begins with insisting, once and for all, that we will never again settle for less than enough. Since there is enough, we have the right and duty to insist upon our share. We needn't hoard and deprive others. But we can assert that our legitimate needs be met.

A life-changing technique I use to responsibly attend to my legitimate needs is carefully and consistently asking myself abundance questions each and every day. This is especially important in times of crisis, disappointment, or loss.

Let's review the challenges facing Melody, Jack, and Allison and see how altering the questions they asked themselves could have altered their experience.

Melody

As you may recall, Melody was about to have dinner with her mother. They had a long-standing pattern of interacting in such a way that Melody was verbally shamed by her mother about her weight. In anxious anticipation of emotional and verbal abuse, Melody began to emotionally and verbally abuse herself, giving no practical thought to self-protection. Working from a scarcity perspective, she had given up hope that she could receive the safety, dignity, and support she legitimately needed.

Imagine that Melody embraced the Perspective of Abundance and insisted that she be provided with adequate safety, dignity, and support. The questions she might ask herself would be, "Is it helpful for me to have dinner with my mother if she insists on shaming me?" "If I decide to have dinner with my mother, what guidelines do I need to set in order to protect myself from abuse?" "If my mother violates these guidelines, what measures do I need to take in order to protect myself or remove myself from danger?"

In response to these positive abundance questions, her mind would naturally create positive answers. She could decide to refuse her mother's invitation for dinner. That is her right. Or, she could decide to take a friend along to help her manage the conversation, sort out how best to respond to certain comments, and to "reality test" the experience on their way home. Perhaps Melody would decide to set a guideline for her mother that declared discussion of her weight off-limits. She could inform her mother that if she were criticized for her eating habits, Melody would simply get up from the table and leave. When based in a personal paradigm that views safety and dignity as available to her, Melody asks and then answers her interior questions in a completely new and life-giving way.

This new perspective is also reflected in the way she might address her weight. Not all weight problems are signs of eating disorders, and not all eating disorders illustrate the same interior dynamic. But for this example, allow me to describe Melody as a woman who was severely deprived of emotional nurturance and support when she was young. Food became a substitute for the mothering she desperately needed. Now, as an adult operating out of a scarcity model, Melody doesn't associate positive feelings with dieting. Instead she experiences dieting as yet another form of deprivation.

When Melody's attention is shifted from her eating patterns toward creating ways to nurture herself, the questions that come to Melody's mind alter dramatically. By insisting on receiving all the nurturance she legitimately needs, Melody begins to ask questions, such as, "How many ways can I receive pleasure today?" "What are the things that delight me about my life?" "What kind of nurturance does my body need today?" "Who could I call during my break who would offer me encouragement?" "What adventure could I have during my lunch hour?" "Who could I invite over this evening who makes me laugh?"

To these abundance questions, Melody's mind might respond by suggesting she take a bubble bath, exercise at the gym, invite over a friend she hasn't seen in several weeks, use her lunch hour for a visit to the local art museum, or arrange for a professional massage after work. As she develops new and satisfying avenues of nurturance, Melody then might ask herself, "What effective, nurturing ways can I slowly lose the weight I want to lose?" As she works from a Perspective of Abundance, dieting can be experienced less as deprivation and more as a way to treat herself and her body with due respect.

Jack

Jack viewed his recent financial disappointment as evidence that there was not enough money in the world for him to have his cut, and, furthermore, as an exposure of his inadequacies. Those who operate from a Perspective of Abundance have a more accurate map of how the world works and, therefore, have more realistic expectations of themselves, others, and life's challenges. Promoting a grace-based approach rather than a shame-based approach, the Perspective of Abundance has no room for failure. Rather, mistakes, disappointments, set-backs, and losses are seen as genuine opportunities for growth and learning.

This is not to say that all these experiences are pleasant, because, of course, many lessons in life can be quite painful. But the presence of pain in our lives does not denote failure. To the contrary, the legitimate pain we experience in life is often the driving force that moves us to a healthier, more loving, more authentic place. For example, those who operate from a Perspective of Abundance know that regardless of the best intentions and highly developed skills, some business ventures pay off and some do not. Any particular outcome is determined by a complex interplay of many components, and we can control only some of them.

Operating from abundance and self-confidence, Jack could ask himself, "What can I learn from this turn of events?" "In my next venture, what will I do differently?" "What parts of this project would I want to repeat?"

Facing the practical consequences of financial pressure, Jack could ask himself, "What can I do in the short run to cover my expenses?" "Who do I know who could help me brainstorm some creative alternatives?" "How can my wife and I work together through this stressful time?" "What special things can we do together that won't be expensive but will be fun and nurturing?" "How can I express my love and appreciation for Marilyn's standing by me all these years?" "What dreams can we create together for the future, once we have gotten past this temporary time of stress?"

In response to these questions, grounded in a belief that financial abundance is available, Jack will greet his wife in a radically different manner from the man we first met who was so convinced that joy was unavailable to him.

Allison

At one time or another, we have all loved someone who did not love us in return. There are few heartbreaks as painful as rejected love. When we operate out of scarcity, we commonly endow any one love relationship with more power and more significance than it actually warrants. We may find ourselves declaring with great drama, "This is the only true love of my life!"; "I could never love another the way I love you!"; or "If I can't have you then I want no one else."

Loss and rejection are painful, no matter what perspective we embrace. When we experience loss from the Perspective of Scarcity, however, we greatly intensify our suffering. Not only do we have to face the realistic loss of the particular person and the practical impact that loss may have on our lives, but we compound our pain by adding *imagined loss*. This *imagined loss* can feel just as painful as realistic loss. In fact, imagined loss sometimes hurts even more, because it feels so large, so global, so uncontrollable. We find ourselves grieving, not only the loss of someone we love, but our belief that we will never love again. Not only do we struggle with the piercing pain of rejection by one person, we expand that pain to include all others, fearing that everyone in the future will reject us as well.

We suffer this enormous pain unnecessarily. No matter how devastating one particular relationship may be, it is extremely unlikely that it will be our last. Regardless of our declarations of unfailing love, most of us, within a matter of time, will indeed love again. How soon we will be able to start over, how deep the wound of rejection penetrates and how long it will take us to heal depend largely on us, not on those who rejected us. Our ex-lovers may "stab us through the heart," but when we operate from a Perspective of Scarcity, we push the "knife" in deeper with our own hands, intensifying our pain and prolonging our time of healing.

Yes, even from a Perspective of Abundance, rejection is painful. But Allison could have decreased her suffering and encouraged healing by asking abundance questions such as, "How can I get the support I need through this time of loss?" "Where can I put the reminders (gifts, cards, pictures) of this relationship out of sight until I am better prepared to deal with them?" "What can I learn from this relationship that will help me love in a healthier way in the future?" "What were the many ways I contributed positively to this relationship?" "How can I best express my anger, disappointment, grief, and frustration over this loss?" "What especially kind things can I do for myself during this time?" "What other men do I know who could remind me that I am an attractive woman?" "Do I need to spend time alone or with others?" "How can I let go of my fantasies and face reality with courage?" "How will I know when I am ready to love again?"

In response to these questions, Allison might find herself calling a close friend and asking her over for the evening for extra support. She could take a weekend off for a spiritual retreat, to walk in the woods and feel the warm love of her Higher Power. A late night dancing with a dear male friend who enjoys loud music and Allison's sense of humor could give her an extra boost during this time of self-doubt. She might ask a friend to help her pack Randy's belongings and return them, so she can avoid another painful confrontation. Perhaps attending a grief seminar or support group will aid Allison's healing. Allison can help herself grow beyond this loss in many, many ways, but only if she believes that healing is possible and that the world holds enough love for her. Randy may not provide the love she wants, but Randy is not the only man available. In a Perspective of Scarcity, Allison may fear Randy is the only man, but in a world of abundance, there will be another love for Allison—and for you.

Asking Questions of Abundance

The Bible tells us "Ask, and you will receive" (John 16:24). Be careful, very careful, about the questions you ask, because you will most definitely receive an answer. If you ask scarcity questions, you will receive scarcity answers, and as a consequence, you will experience only life's losses, limitations, and sadness. Conversely, if you ask from a Perspective of Abundance, then abundance you will receive. There is enough for all of us, so please don't settle for anything less than enough. You can have everything you need. All you have to do is ask.

3

Enlarge the Limits of Your Enjoyment Comfort Zone

In honor of my last birthday, a group of my friends gathered at a local restaurant, donned silly hats, ate a lot of pizza, and danced until midnight. Since those in attendance were some of my favorite people in the world, I was thoroughly enjoying myself. When it came time for the cake, however, two cakes rather than one appeared on the table. I realized that two of my friends had brought cakes, and I felt uncomfortable.

"Oh, no," I thought to myself, "somehow I should have planned this better." Having two cakes was somehow an illustration of my inability to organize a proper party. I was concerned that my friends would feel put out since one of the cakes was purchased unnecessarily. As I cut the cakes and passed out pieces, I worried whether one of the cakes would be preferred over the other, making my friends feel like they brought an inferior cake. My worries went on and on, further and further into absurdity, changing my enjoyment into distress.

Later that night I realized receiving the extra cake was outside my Enjoyment Comfort Zone. I was fundamentally embarrassed by having two cakes at my party, because while one cake seemed appropriate, I didn't feel I deserved two cakes. The second cake was a trigger for shame, rather than an opportunity to enjoy an additional symbol of nurturance from my friends (to say nothing of another great tasting cake!).

We all have an Enjoyment Comfort Zone, a circle we draw around ourselves within which we are able to experience pleasure. For some this circle is very small. We permit ourselves little enjoyment, allow only a few positive experiences into our lives and may even punish ourselves if too many good things start to happen. We often define our Enjoyment Comfort Zone with unconscious dimensions, rooted in whether we operate from a Perspective of Scarcity or a Perspective of Abundance.

Scarcity and Our Spiritual Wound

The Perspective of Scarcity originates in a deep spiritual wound many of us suffered from childhood abuse or neglect. Regardless of what we may claim to believe, many of us unconsciously believe that God does not pay attention to our needs, nor is there enough in the universe to supply our needs. Some believe God is cruel, wanting us to put everyone else's needs ahead of our own. In fact, there have been times when I thought that God was actually pleased when I suffered deprivation or abuse, that my suffering was somehow godly and enjoying life's goodness was selfish and sinful.

We must not, so the Perspective of Scarcity claims, ever be selfish, because when we take what we need, we steal from others. There isn't enough, so the lie goes, for everyone to have what they need. The Perspective of Scarcity promotes a view of God who deprives us of enough time, enough rest, enough laughter, enough love . . . enough of anything except the never-ending obligation to serve others.

At the core of all addictions is a spiritual wound that results in our losing faith in a God who loves us, in a world that nurtures us, and in a spiritual process that results in resurrection. Those of us who have been spiritually wounded operate from a view of scarcity, and unconsciously we value deprivation over fulfillment. We may actually take a sense of pride and satisfaction in the abuse we suffer or the deprivation we endure. As a consequence, we are unable to experience the love and nurturance God offers and the rebirth that is possible. We must face this spiritual wound and embrace the truth: *we have a God who loves us, enjoys us, and heals us.*

I travel all over this country presenting workshops, and rarely do I meet people who feel that they are experiencing enough love, nurturance, peace of mind, financial security, sense of safety, passion, and pleasure. I firmly believe that God provides us with all we need in every area, but because of the limits of our Enjoyment Comfort Zone, we are unable to experience what is right there before us. When we are offered positive experiences that are outside our Enjoyment Comfort Zone, we cannot enjoy them. In fact, we often do not even see them.

When we do not believe that God delights in us, we do not delight in ourselves. We draw a tight circle around ourselves, repelling positive experiences. We cut ourselves off from any degree of pleasure that exceeds our unconscious standard of what we believe we deserve. If some pleasurable experience slips through, we duly punish ourselves in one manner or another.

When operating from the Perspective of Scarcity, we experience these positive opportunities as negative. We may feel guilty for taking too much and being selfish. We may experience a phone call from a friend as a drain on our time rather than an offer for support. Sometimes we feel embarrassed for attracting too much attention to ourselves. Or, as at my birthday party, I experienced the second cake, intended as a positive opportunity for additional nurturance, as something negative and shameful.

The Twelve Steps assert that we have a Higher Power, able to restore us to sanity. I believe sanity is based on a balanced experience of reality, encompassing both death and rebirth, grief and celebration. Far too often, unfortunately, in recovery we focus on only half of the picture, on the death and the grief. Rebirth and celebration are viewed as luxuries we have been forbidden to enjoy. As our spiritual wounds heal and we come to believe God truly enjoys us, our self-esteem increases. As we enlarge our self-esteem the boundaries of our Enjoyment Comfort Zone are similarly enlarged.

In fact, I believe one way to assess the level of your self-esteem is to see how much pleasure you allow into your life. Look at your schedule and see for yourself. How much time is devoted to the care of others and how much to your own nurturance? Are you busy working endless hours or do you allow adequate time for play? How many of your relationships are one-sided with the nurturance coming solely from you? How often do you allow friends and family to support and care for you? At my birthday party, I realized that my self-esteem was high enough to enjoy celebrating with my friends, but too low to allow two cakes worth of nurturance. At that time in my life, my self-esteem and, therefore, my Enjoyment Comfort Zone could accommodate only one cake.

It is critical to identify the boundaries of your Enjoyment Comfort Zone because, in doing so, you may find that many of your negative experiences are in fact positive opportunities that are being overlooked, misinterpreted, or repelled.

Unconscious Associations and the Perspective of Scarcity

Because many of us operate out of a Perspective of Scarcity, we make negative unconscious associations with experiences that could otherwise be pleasurable. Our unconscious minds are continually defining experiences as positive or negative, sometimes in rather off ways. For example, a good friend of mind refuses to eat dill pickles. In fact, she can't stand the sight of them because when she was a little girl she became quite ill after eating a dill pickle on a hot summer afternoon. Every time she catches a glimpse of a dill pickle, her stomach gets queasy and she begins to re-experience that awful day. Dill pickles are definitely not in her Enjoyment Comfort Zone.

I, on the other hand, thoroughly enjoy eating dill pickles because when I bite into a crisp pickle, I think of Disneyland. Each time I leave the theme park, I buy a large dill pickle at one of the shops on Main Street. Eating pickles conjures up feelings of relaxation, that tired happiness I feel after a long, enjoyable day. In fact, my positive association to dill pickles is so strong that in times of sadness I sometimes buy a dill pickle just to give myself an emotional lift.

Like many other things in life, dill pickles have the potential to be sources of pain or pleasure, depending on the associations we have stored in our unconscious minds. We may have no conscious memory of these experiences and be unaware of our associations. We merely find some things to be enjoyable while others are upsetting or even painful. Perhaps when you were a teenager your friends made fun as you tried out new dance steps. That experience may be forgotten, but now you find the prospect of spending a night dancing more frightening than inviting. Maybe as a child swimming with your friends, you were teased and pushed beneath the surface of the water. Struggling for air, fearing for your life, you may have come to distrust the water. And now, you turn down the offer of a day swimming at the beach, which could be an opportunity for pleasure. For you, however, water sports aren't within your Enjoyment Comfort Zone.

When we were teenagers, my girlfriend and I went out several nights in a row to social functions. Thursday evening, her father told her she couldn't join me again for a night out. My friend explained that her homework was done, the outing would be chaperoned, and we would be home at a reasonable hour. "None of that matters," her father said. "I still don't want you to go. I'm afraid you are having too much fun, and I want you to learn that life isn't fun. It is hard and difficult."

Many of us have been taught that having "too much fun" is bad. Rooted in the Perspective of Scarcity, things get turned upside down, pleasure gets linked to pain ("Why are you sitting around playing that game when there's work to do? I'm ashamed of you!") while pain or deprivation somehow is associated with a positive outcome ("I'm glad to see you working rather than wasting your time listening to that awful music"). Because of the dysfunction of our families, we may have unconsciously learned to associate pleasure, not with feelings of nurturance, enjoyment, and safety, but with guilt, fear, shame, and danger. Now that we are adults, our attempts to enjoy ourselves are often undermined by our unconscious fears and negative associations.

Since the Perspective of Scarcity has permeated our society for many generations, our attitudes about work and leisure have been deeply affected and distorted. When operating from the Perspective of Scarcity, we are unable to see that the pleasure play provides us, as children and as adults, is of intrinsic value. Sadly enough, pleasure, for its own sake, is rarely valued in this society. In fact, pleasure is often distrusted. As Robert K. Johnston points out in *The Christian at Play*, Western culture has been strongly influenced by Augustine, a theologian of the fourth century, who believed that true spirituality was a "conversion from a life of play. To him, even eating was sinful if done in a spirit of pleasure. . . . It is often thought that in play one risks being uninvolved and irresponsible. The evils of play's misuses have been judged more severely than the perversions of work. It is safer to spend one's time in 'serious' activity than to enter into 'frivolity.'"[1]

As a workaholic and codependent, I do not remember being told that the many hours I worked were shameful or being confronted for over-investing in helping others. Oh, no, to the contrary, I was rewarded for my addiction. Workaholism, perhaps the addiction most hostile to a lifestyle that incorporates a healthy attitude toward play and pleasure, is more often admired than confronted in this society.

In *Confessions of a Workaholic*, Wayne E. Oates writes, "This land of ours is full of workaholics. This workaholic's way of life is considered in America to be at one and the same time (a) a religious value, (b) a form of patriotism, (c) the way to win friends and influence people, and (d) the way to be healthy, wealthy, and wise. . . . [The workaholic] is a sort of paragon of virtue . . . the one chosen as 'the most likely to succeed.'"[2]

For those caught in the Perspective of Scarcity, work is valued while pleasure is distrusted. Work that is excessive, addictive, demanding, back-breaking, or even health-breaking is endowed with even more positive associations. The more painful the project, the more it is valued.

From this perspective, play and pleasure can only be considered profitable if those activities, in some way, advance one's work. Walter Kerr, in *The Decline of Pleasure*, insightfully points out that we are "compelled to read for profit, party for contacts, lunch for contracts, bowl for unity, drive for mileage, gamble for charity, go out for the evening for the greater glory of the municipality, and stay home for the weekend to rebuild the house."[3]

Those blinded by the Perspective of Scarcity are unable to see the benefits of pleasure for their own sake, which enhance our quality of life. More tragic, perhaps, is the inability to recognize that beyond the sheer value of enjoyment, the lack of play is detrimental to our well-being in all areas, emotional, spiritual, physical, intellectual, and social.

For the past several years, I have worked out of my home as an author, speaker, and consultant. Being a night person, I tend to work in the afternoons and evenings rather than the mornings. I frequently receive calls in the morning and am awakened by teasing, shame-based comments like, "Wow, I wish I could stay home and sleep all day. But I have to work for a living."

Once I would launch into extensive descriptions of the hours I had worked the previous day, feeling the need to justify myself as a worthwhile person by my productivity. As I have embraced the Perspective of Abundance, I have released more of my shame. Rather than defend myself according to a distorted work ethic, I am becoming more comfortable with responding, "Yeah, it's true. I'm learning to enjoy life."

When we operate out of the Perspective of Abundance, the benefits of play seem obvious. The distorted associations of the Perspective of Scarcity are revised. It is then possible to see the benefits of both types of activities, work—activity that has value by virtue of its end results, as well as play—activity that has value for its own sake.

If we do not recognize how our unconscious minds have been filled with distorted associations that pit play and work against each other rather than allowing these activities to work hand in hand for an enjoyable and productive life, we will continue to sabotage our opportunities for genuine pleasure and life-giving play. We may find more comfort in retreating to our offices to work through the evening than in playing a game with our children. Propelled by the need to be needed, we may actually feel at home when dashing from meeting to meeting while finding ourselves agitated by an afternoon off. We only work within our Enjoyment Comfort Zone, while pleasurable activities will, in fact, trigger more anxiety, confusion, and discomfort than we can tolerate.

Associations we have made to pain and pleasure can be even more distorted if we were victims of abuse or deprivation. If we were abused sexually as children, the touch of an adult lover can be quite frightening. Struggling with strong feelings of emotional deprivation, we may link excessive pleasure to a piece of chocolate. We may associate the hope of approval with a relentless work schedule, finding pleasure in self-destruction. In order to numb the pain, we actually intensify our suffering.

We can trace our attachment to many addictive behaviors to our mis-associating pleasure with dangerous or painful experiences. An alcoholic links pleasure to drinking, in spite of the blackouts, the vomiting, the loss of employment, the humiliation, and the ruined relationships. Likewise, the food addict links pleasure to excessive eating, regardless of the health hazards, the social stigma of being overweight, and the physical limitations experienced. As a codependent, I associated pleasure with an exhausting work schedule and depriving myself of the nurturance I needed. Many of us have included inappropriate experiences inside our Enjoyment Comfort Zone.

Properly defining our Enjoyment Comfort Zone entails two aspects. First, we must exclude detrimental experiences, those activities that are usually addictive in nature. Second, we must link genuinely nurturing and beneficial experiences to pleasure, thereby giving ourselves permission to enjoy our lives.

Repairing Our Mis-Associations

When operating from a Perspective of Scarcity, we are always looking for someone to blame for our discomfort. As a single woman, I often felt there was not enough love in my life. For years I looked for love, as if hunting down a shrewd and untameable prey. Like many, I blamed my singleness on the men I met, complaining bitterly that "there just aren't any good men around." But then I watched other women meet good men, fall in love, and get married. "Humph!" I stewed to myself, "so much for that theory."

As I moved through recovery and therapy, I began to see the dynamics I had picked up from my family that ill-prepared me for successful coupling. So, I shifted from blaming men to blaming my parents. Everything that went wrong in my life, as far as I was concerned, was their fault. Blaming other people for my plight put me in the role of Victim and undermined my sense of power and any feelings of optimism. Instead, I felt angry and defeated.

The spiral of blame continued as I shifted the blame again, from others to myself. But blaming myself wasn't any more helpful than blaming others, as the very act of blaming leaves us powerless. Instead of aiding in meeting my legitimate needs for love, sex, and companionship, my self-esteem was further undermined. I cruelly criticized myself for being inadequate, unlovable, and unattractive.

As I have slowly embraced a Perspective of Abundance, I have become more able to let go of my need to blame, and have instead learned to discern who to hold responsible for what. Rather than dismiss the entire gender, I am learning to differentiate between men who are capable of loving me and those who are not. By accurately assessing the limitations I inherited from my family, I can address these issues directly, rather than lapse into a pervasive and helpless "my life is ruined forever because of what happened to me way back when" attitude. I am learning to identify the ways I have indeed undermined my opportunities for love, because I unconsciously linked a stronger negative than positive association to intimacy. Consciously I claimed to want love in my life. Unconsciously, however, I battled against any man getting too close.

For example, recently I received a call from a man to whom I had been attracted for some time. After weeks of wishing he would ask me out, the phone rang and his voice was on the line, saying exactly what I had hoped he would say. When I hung up the phone, was I thrilled? Was I confident? Was I ready to go out on my date with optimistic anticipation? No.

I immediately called a friend and vented my fear of rejection, my shame over a couple of rather silly jokes I'd made, and my rage at how I anticipated he would mistreat me. Then, she and I began to laugh as we both saw how oddly I was responding to getting what I had wanted. Clearly, I associated the offer of fun, intimacy, and, at the very least, an enjoyable evening, with some very dark and painful emotions.

Take a look at the areas of deprivation you experience. What are the boundaries of your Enjoyment Comfort Zone? Do you derive pleasure from genuinely healthy activities? Or are you drawn toward anxiety, addiction, and loss like a moth to a flame? Take time to identify your hidden fears. What are the unconscious associations you have made that sabotage your opportunities to play? How do you feel when you have free time? Thrilled or anxious? Grateful or guilty? As these associations are properly realigned, your Enjoyment Comfort Zone will expand to include genuinely helpful, nurturing, and pleasurable experiences. I am finding this quite true in my own life. As I face my fear of intimacy, I am able to recognize and embrace offers of love I previously overlooked or rejected. What are your fears? Isn't it time to allow yourself all the joy God has available for you?

4

Acknowledge the Value
of Play

On one of my speaking trips to New England one fall, I took
a van from the airport to the hotel in which I would be staying.
The ride was delightful, for it gave me the chance to enjoy the
glorious reds, yellows, and pinks of the fall leaves.

As the van drove through a residential section, I spied two
young boys, brothers perhaps, one around seven and the other
around ten, who were raking the leaves that had fallen in their
front yard. The older boy was laboring with a scowl on his face,
dutifully raking the leaves into a large pile. His younger
brother, however, practically danced across the yard, adding
a few leaves to the pile. As the van turned the corner, I saw
the seven-year-old leap onto the pile of leaves, tossing them
over his head in delight.

Play vs. Work

Child development experts tell us that play is a voluntary
and absorbing activity engaged in for the enjoyment it gives,
without consideration of the end result. Work, on the other

hand, is an activity performed, not necessarily for enjoyment, but because of the anticipated end result. Drudgery, work that is experienced as unpleasant, has no element in common with play as it is involuntary, goal-oriented, and often non-engaging.

Any activity could be considered play or work. What differentiates work from play is the attitude the participant has regarding his or her involvement. The young boys I spotted from the van were both raking leaves. However, the two boys were experiencing the same activity quite differently. The older boy undoubtedly was working while the younger boy was playing.

We live in a society that gives us mixed messages about the value placed on play and work. As a culture highly influenced by the Puritan Work Ethic, we have been raised with sayings such as "idle hands will find some mischief to do" and "a rolling stone gathers no moss." As children, we were also told that "all work and no play makes Jack a dull boy." Many of us have internalized conflicting and even contradictory messages regarding work and play. As one child development expert points out, "The live-for-the-moment aspect of [play], combined with the fact that play arises spontaneously from within the child and is not [adult] determined, lends an air of frivolity to it that may lead work-oriented persons to assume it is not worthwhile."[1]

The Value of Play

We now know that play is critical to a child's proper development by helping the child comprehend and gain a sense of mastery over the environment. Even though a child may be motivated to play out of the sheer enjoyment of the activity, the process of play helps the child develop into a more competent and healthy individual. There are at least seven benefits to play.

Creativity Development

Anything is possible for a child at play!

A stick can become a magic wand able to grant any wish imaginable, or it can be a knight's trusty sword. A rock can be transformed into a marker for buried treasure or be used to build a fort deep in the dangerous wilderness. With a little imagination, a piece of paper can be folded into a crown to be worn by the queen, cut into pieces to create a colorful mosaic, or contain secret messages for fellow spies hiding behind enemy lines. Child development specialist Joanne Hendrick writes, "Play, which arises from within, expresses the child's personal, unique response to the environment. It is inherently a self-expressive activity that draws richly on the child's power of imagination."[2]

Perhaps the most tragic attitude I confront in the people who attend my seminars is the lack of hope that something new or wonderful could happen to them. Cut off from their childlike imagination, these adults suffer greatly from the resulting sense of helplessness. They tell me things like:

> I don't know what to do with my life. I used to have dreams, but now nothing seems possible. So much of my life has been wasted. I can't find love anywhere. I've tried and tried, but all of my relationships end miserably.

> I'm working night and day and still can't seem to make ends meet. I'm stuck. There's nothing I can do.

> I know I need to take better care of myself, but how? I can't afford a weekly massage, let alone regular therapy or even a vacation.

These kinds of statements tell me that these people have lost contact with their own creative nature. Oddly enough, many of these people may be highly skilled at discovering creative alternatives when engaged in helping others. But in their own lives, they feel they've tried everything only to be disappointed.

Most of the time when I question these people further, I find that the "everything" they've tried has been one over-used, outdated strategy. For example, Eddie, who considers himself a loser at love, insists there are no women in his town, yet refuses to attend singles groups, join activity clubs, or invest in a personal ad. "That's not for me!" he insists. Apparently what is for him is sitting alone each weekend, wondering where all the good women are. Unless Eddie changes his strategy, meets new women, and invites them home, they are not going to magically appear in his living room. Like many people I meet, Eddie repeatedly uses a familiar but self-defeating approach to getting his needs met. He refuses to update his reality map.

June, an attractive mother of three, is unhappy in her job and her marriage. June's strategy is simple; she is waiting. She is waiting for her husband to change and the right job to appear, feeling that there is nothing she can do to get what she wants out of life. Deeply entrenched in a traditional perspective, June assumes her task as a woman is to wait for her prince, her job, and her happiness to come to her.

Wayne, an overweight man who came up to talk after a workshop, told me that his doctor has warned him that he is in danger of heart disease. "But I've got a business to run and a family to support," he complained. "Those gyms are too expensive to join and, besides, no one is going to pay me to play for a living. The competition is too strong these days."

All of these people are holding on to outdated personal paradigms, channeling their creativity into cultivating deprivation rather than cultivating abundance. Because we are created in the image of God, we are born into this world as creative beings. If that innate creativity is nurtured and encouraged through play when we are children, we will continue to joyously create a life we enjoy living as adults. Of course, the opposite is also true. If our play is disrupted, or taken from us, through childhood abuse or deprivation, we lose faith in our ability to come up with new alternatives. We become fearful of exploring new avenues, and see life's limitations and scarcity rather than its potential and abundance.

How do you use your creativity? Do you come up with ways you can do without what you need, or ways you can get what you need? Do you devise excuses for your unhappiness, or invest energy in making changes in your life? Are you expending more energy blaming others, or inviting others to join you in new adventures? Do you trust you can devise a variety of fun ideas for your next vacation, or have you given up hope on having any time to play?

If you have lost hope, I suspect you can trace that loss to your childhood. Remember, like every infant, you came into this world with an innate curiosity and a confident creative spirit. If you have lost access to your imagination and you can no longer see life's possibilities, it is important to look back in time and locate when, how, and where your childhood playtime was violated and your imagination stifled.

Physical Development

From the gurgling delight of an infant just discovering his toes to the ecstatic cheer of an athlete winning her first gold medal, physical activity can serve as a tremendous avenue of self-exploration and challenge development. At each developmental stage, physical play activities give children an irreplaceable opportunity to explore the world, develop a sense of mastery, and promote a healthier body.

Young children, whose play is usually solitary and exploratory, enjoy discovering and playing with parts of their own bodies. For toddlers, physical play such as hopping, rolling on the floor, and bobbing to music serves to strengthen growing muscles and facilitate coordination. As the child grows older, physical activities become more complex, such as climbing, swinging, playing ball, swimming, dancing or skating.

Children not allowed to engage in physical play can lack muscle development, hand-eye coordination, cardiovascular strength, or over-all health. This invaluable avenue of physical development and self-exploration can be disrupted in a variety of ways.

Hanna cannot recall playing as a girl except for recess at

school because she had to hurry home each day after school to help care for her brothers and sisters. Since her father, a minister and workaholic, was rarely at home to help with the chores, her mother relied heavily on Hanna's assistance. Hanna was expected to watch her siblings as they played, but was never allowed to play herself.

Frank didn't play with other children because they made fun of him. They called him "Four-Eyed Frankie" because he wore thick glasses and had trouble catching a ball. Rather than endure the shame, Frank withdrew from physical play and retreated into the private games he made up in his head.

Tina once loved to run and could beat any boy in her class in a race. She sadly remembers sitting on the side of the playground, immobilized by a cast on her leg. She told everyone she had fallen to protect her father from getting into trouble. Tina didn't want anyone to know her father was beating her mother, and when Tina tried to stop him he pushed her down the stairs. Even now, that leg bothers her when she jogs, so she doesn't try to compete in community marathons.

Jose remembers concentrating until the sweat poured down his face. Gripping the bat until his fingers ached, he stood at home plate waiting for the pitch. The thought of his dad watching him in the stands twisted his stomach into knots. "You're the only one with any talent on this team," his father had told him. "It's up to you if this team makes it into the finals." Jose swallowed hard, repeating to himself over and over and over, "I gotta get a hit. I gotta get a hit."

I remember once playing freely as a child. But as I grew older, my playtime was disrupted, not by my family but by the religious subculture in which I was raised. I was taught to distrust the "flesh," and so I developed an animosity toward my own body. In my misguided effort to please God, I conformed to this distortion, distinguishing spiritual pursuits over physical enjoyment, valuing intellectual accomplishment over athletic development. Like all children, I began life at one with my body. It was not long, however, before I not only separated my "self" from my body, but began to view my body with suspicion and even as a source of deceit or danger.

In these ways and others, children can be deprived of the irreplaceable opportunity of joyful physical play. Most of us have suffered from some sense of separation from our bodies, some of us by being physically prevented from play activities while others of us withdrew because of shaming or other emotionally abusive experiences associated with our bodies.

How do you relate to your body? Is it with ease and a sense of satisfaction, or with disgust and shame? Are you physically active, finding joy in the sheer pleasure of movement, or do you shy away from making a spectacle of yourself? When you try a new sport are you anxious to get it right or are you thrilled at the exploration of something new, regardless of your level of skill? Do you provide yourself with a balanced, high-energy diet, or do you deprive or over-indulge your appetite? Do you honor your body through regular and reasonable exercise, or have you let yourself go? If you feel alienated from your body, you may neglect your body's needs through deprivation or, at the other extreme, because you are highly competitive you may force your body to perform at excessive levels. Carefully assess your relationship with your body. If you are out of synch, it could be because your playtime, which was meant to be free, engaging and pleasurable, was instead charged with fear, violence, or shame.

Intellectual Development

Toy manufacturers have long recognized the educational value of play. Often the marketing of a toy will have a dual focus, to convince a child the toy will be fun and to assure mom and dad the toy will aid in the child's intellectual development. Perhaps the most popular children's television show of all time, "Sesame Street" cleverly united the elements of fun with the task of learning. Play, regardless of its type, teaches children something new about the world around them and about themselves.

Katie made mud pies in her backyard and learned about the

soil, water, and how to use molds. Fred made model cars, thereby learning about glue, paint, and the principles of design. By splashing her little hands in the bath, Peggie discovered a lot about water, waves, and maybe even something about how to get mom wet in the process. Through collecting stamps, Craig learned about counting, sorting, and countries that are far away.

If Katie had been punished for getting dirty rather than allowed to explore the mysteries of her backyard, she might not have become a grower of prize orchids. A major source of joy in her adult life could have been missed. If Fred hadn't been encouraged in his model building, he might not have developed the skills he now uses daily as an engineer. Peggie's mother might have scolded her, rather than laughing and sharing in the fun when water sprayed around the bathroom. If shamed, Peggie might have become fearful of the water and today might not be a water aerobics teacher for the senior center in her town. While his stamp collection is stored now with his other childhood toys, had it not been for the hours of gazing at colorful images of far off lands, Craig might not have become interested in international travel.

All of these children engaged in play, not because they thought it would help their intellectual development, but because it was fun. Yet, as children and later as adults, each benefitted greatly when these learning experiences were incorporated into and utilized for their enjoyment of life.

Take an honest look at your own life. Do you find this world boring or intriguing? Is it dull or full of mystery, scary or inviting? Do you retain your childhood curiosity or have you become jaded and disinterested? If you have disengaged from the process of learning, quite possibly somewhere along the way your natural and necessary need to play was disrupted.

This is not to say that you are not intelligent. One's IQ does not relate to one's intellectual interest in the world. To the contrary, some researchers claim that we use only 10 percent of our brain's capacities. No matter how smart we may be, I believe that every adult can be fully engaged with life intellectually, whether that capacity is focused on memorizing baseball statistics or calculus formulas, reading fascinating fiction or researching historical documents, critiquing a foreign film or assessing recent political developments. If you do not draw pleasure from intellectual activity of some kind, if you do not find this world absolutely teeming with curious, wonderful, and intriguing mysteries, you may have been robbed of joyful, adventurous playtime when you were a child.

Psychological Development

Perhaps one of the most important by-products of play is the opportunity to explore, develop, and get to know one's self. Initially, infants do not differentiate between themselves and the world around them, assuming their hunger is the world's hunger and their delight is the world's delight. As they discover their fingers, toes, arms, and legs, and watch Mommy come, go, and return again, they make distinctions between themselves and others. Play provides an invaluable avenue of proper self-insight and definition.

Small children learn about their own abilities through playing with blocks, sand, water, and other objects. As they master each level of achievement, children gain confidence and positive self-esteem. When a child imagines something he or she may want to create, problem solving skills develop as the child uses pieces of yarn instead of string, and straws and pencils become a metal rod. As the creative juices flow, children learn that their goals can be reached in more ways than one. Accordingly, the task, whether drawing a picture, creating a bird house, or writing a story, helps children to better define who they are and how they fit into this complex world.

Older children often participate in social or team activities. Again, play offers them chances to develop psychologically as they compare their abilities with those of others. They develop a realistic concept of self.

Children who are made to feel fearful of failure, however, may be reluctant to explore and try new approaches. These children are often raised by perfectionistic parents who view their children's exploration as possibly reflecting poorly on themselves. Unable to see their children as separate beings, perfectionistic parents tend to undermine their children's development of healthy self-esteem. One of the ways this damage occurs is by the parent invading the child's playtime, turning care-free play into a fearful experience of possible failure. Play, in order to be play, is child-centered, free, and absorbing. Activity that is regularly interrupted by adults, infused with anxiety or performance expectations, is no longer play.

What were your playtimes like when you were a child? Were you given the opportunity to freely explore, make mistakes, try again, devise alternate plans? Were you allowed to test your abilities and feel good about your accomplishments? Or were you pushed to succeed, excel, and make your parents proud? When you showed your play creations to your parents or teachers, were you given a response that strengthened your self-esteem or one that undermined your confidence? Were your drawings proudly displayed on the refrigerator or tossed in the trash?

How would you assess your psychological stability now? Are you clear about who you are, what you like, what you are good at, and where you want to focus your energy? Or do you more often feel confused, hesitant, or lost in the complexity of life? What did you learn about yourself during playtime those many years ago?

Emotional Development

Recently I was riding in the passenger seat of a van driven by Annette, a friend of mine and the mother of two children. In the seats behind us, her children and a couple of their friends were playing car games, calling out to each other and regularly exploding with delighted bursts of laughter. Annette smiled wearily at me and asked philosophically, "Why is it, while other people complain about losing their hearing as they get older, I get all the more sensitive to noise?" We laughed as another flood of raucous enthusiasm exploded behind us.

Play offers children a contained and (for the most part) socially acceptable way to express emotion. I believe that feelings are, in part, energy meant to move us toward some course of action. Feelings of love may motivate us to hug, comfort, or kiss someone. Fear may warn us of danger and prompt us to run or fight back. Softer feelings, such as contentment or satisfaction, may soothe us to relax or enjoy the moment. Or more agitating feelings such as outrage or frustration may catapult us into action.

Children express a variety of emotions through play. A doll may be hit one moment and cuddled the next as a child expresses rage and compassion. Kicking a ball across the school yard may replace the urge to kick a living being. Drawing with bright colors may denote happiness or hope while scribbling with blacks and browns and dark purple may express sadness, despair, or disappointment.

Children express emotions through play in so many ways. Some release energy through their voices by singing, screaming, laughing, or whispering. Others learn to express themselves through music or rhythm with simple activities, such as hitting two sticks together, clapping, or playing a tambourine. Expressing feelings through music can take complex forms, such as playing a musical instrument or singing in harmony. Energy can also be released through large muscle activities such as running, climbing, team sports, bike riding, skating, or skiing. Feelings can be expressed symbolically through play as well as through painting, drawing, or model construction.

Family scenes can be recreated and explored through a variety of make-believe games including doll play, war games, super hero role play, or pretending to be a favorite movie star. Through make-believe games, children who may feel powerless can, for a time, feel the thrill of mastery through their imaginations in play. They can also use play that is free and uncontaminated by interference from adults to balance the day-to-day pressure most children feel to conform to parental demands and social norms. Play, effectively utilized, gives children chances to explore, express, and gain a sense of mastery over their own emotional lives. Self-expression in socially acceptable avenues is the natural by-product of a child allowed to play in age-appropriate ways.

Children who are raised in families where all feelings are provided a legitimate avenue of expression are able to grow up capable of finding socially acceptable yet authentic avenues of communication. Many of us, however, were allowed to express only some of our feelings directly. In those families where children were to be seen and not heard, expression of any feeling at all was taboo.

How would you assess your emotional well-being? Do you have a variety of socially acceptable and satisfying ways to express your feelings? Or are there times you are unsure of what you are feeling, let alone know how to express your emotions? Those of us who as adults are cut off from our feelings and lack mastery over proper expression of emotion are often those who were cut off from expressive play as children.

Social Development

The potential social value of play is enormous as children are confronted with that loathsome concept of sharing. Few wars have been waged with the intensity felt by toddlers, screeching at top-lung capacity, as they fight for possession of a favorite toy.

As children grow older, team games provide opportunities to learn cooperation, sharing, and proper boundary setting. Conflicts can teach children how to properly express aggression and develop plans of compromise. They learn skills needed in becoming good losers or good winners through a variety of games and sports.

Dramatic play, or make-believe, wherein children take on various roles such as mom, dad, teacher, cowboy, super hero, or villain, gives children chances to learn social roles through imitation. Such play helps children develop empathy by experiencing someone else's role. Through many forms of play, children can become adept at a variety of social skills, learn society's expectations, and establish their own sex role definitions. Children can learn to manage power through negotiation and compromise.

A glance around us, however, illustrates that we live in a world of great social turmoil. One look in any bookstore confirms that relationships, specifically relating to romance and intimacy, are major issues of interest. Watch the news on any given night and you will be confronted with horrible stories of violence, racial conflict, and political unrest. Go to a Twelve Step meeting and you will hear tale after tale of abuse and neglect. We are clearly a world of people who have major difficulties getting along with each other. I suspect we once were all children who were not allowed to play freely. Rather than learning to work out our conflicts symbolically on the playground, we now battle quite literally on the war field.

How do you view the success of your relationships? Are they balanced? Do you receive the same measure of nurturance that you provide? Or, have you fallen into the same trap I have of giving away a great deal more than you receive? Have you developed the capacity to genuinely love someone else? Or do you view relationships as primarily a place to get what you want? Do you experience others as separate from yourself, or do you get your feelings lost in theirs? When people express their unique feelings are you able to empathize, or do you find their feelings somewhat threatening? All of these issues, whether problematic or happily resolved at this time in your life, can be traced back, in part, to the success or failure of your childhood play opportunities. Those afternoons playing with your friends, or left isolated by yourself, may have been more important than you've ever dreamed.

Moral Development

"What are the rules?" I heard eight-year-old Patti ask her brother Steve as she picked up the playing cards. As he rattled off the guidelines, I turned to their mother and sighed, "I wish the rules of life were that easy to discern."

What are the rules? Are there any? Do you believe the world has an intrinsic moral structure, or is it all up for grabs? A very common problem plaguing those of us in recovery is the loss of moral grounding. Confused by the double, triple, and quadruple messages we may have received from the adults in our lives when we were children, many of us have lost a sense of right and wrong.

Not that our families had no rules, oh, there were plenty, but the rules in a dysfunctional family are usually convoluted, unspoken, and unfair. "Do as I say and not as I do" may have been one of your family rules as your mother nagged you about cleaning your room while the house was a mess. Claudia Black, in *It Will Never Happen to Me*, identified three rules common to alcoholic families: Don't Trust, Don't Talk, and Don't Feel.[3]

A child who plays within the confines of clear and fair rules has the opportunity to internalize a clear and fair moral structure. Those of us given mixed messages may intend to do what is right, but get lost along the way. Many in recovery have been addicted to substances or processes that were powerful enough to overwhelm a commitment to a moral course of action. We may have meant to quit drinking, but then lied to cover up our alcoholism. We may value honesty, but have cheated a business associate because of our compulsion to succeed. Committed to social justice, we may have given our emotional resources away in selfless service, only to find nurturance in the bed of a married co-worker.

What did you learn through your playtime as a child? Were the rules clear or confused? Were you a good scout, learning to be brave, honest, and true? Or did your scout leader abuse your trust, leaving you confused and hurting? Did you learn to win by mastering the task or did you cheat? How you conduct yourself as an adult has been strongly influenced by the games you played when you were a child.

Recovering the Value of Play

With so many benefits to play, how could anyone doubt its value? Do we feel we have outgrown the usefulness of play now that we are adults? Perhaps. I suspect, however, that many of us have not incorporated a healthy sense of play and enjoyment into our adult lives because our childhood playtimes were disrupted or taken from us altogether. Many of us do not know how to play as adults because we never learned to play as children.

Many of us who were raised in dysfunctional families were robbed of the chance to play and, therefore, our development was disrupted. Are these opportunities forever lost to us? Fortunately, within our unconscious minds lives the child we once were, a child who can lead us back in time and teach us, at last, how to play.

5

Open Yourself to Your Inner Child

The red Irish setter stood nose to nose with two-year-old Jenny, eyeing her ice cream cone with great interest. The large dog lunged forward to snatch the ice cream, causing the little girl to lose her balance and her hold on the cone. We heard a shriek from across the yard, and looked up in time to see legs, dog fur, and ice cream flying. Mel, Jenny's father, raced across the yard and quickly snatched the dog, which was licking the last drippings of ice cream from the ground. He put the dog into his yard while I comforted in my arms the crying two-year-old who was both frightened by the dog's assault and frustrated over the loss of her treat. She was dependent upon us to protect her from the dog and to provide her with another chance at happiness, which at that moment meant going into the kitchen for another scoop of ice cream.

Our Inner Child

Like Jenny, we were all once children who were legitimately dependent upon older, larger, more capable people for our protection, well-being, and happiness. If our legitimate needs weren't met, however, they didn't just go away. They remained. And those unmet needs caused many of us to become stuck psychologically, as if frozen in time, feeling very much in need, and quite incapable of taking care of ourselves.

Often referred to as our inner child, the part of ourselves that is stuck back in time lives inside us *as if* we were still children. These inner children don't have psychological access to adult capabilities or insight. It is easy to understand that Jenny was too small to protect herself from the family pet, incapable of opening the refrigerator door, and too short to reach the ice cream and give herself pleasure. However, it can be more difficult to see why we, as adults, can't protect or nurture ourselves. But, those of us who were injured through abuse or neglect may have parts of ourselves that are still very much like Jenny: small, weak, and incapable of nurturing ourselves. When we get into our inner child space, we just don't have the skill to do those things we need done.

All we know is that we feel scared and vulnerable, desperate to be held and comforted. Listen quietly and you might hear your inner child ask, "Why won't anyone give me what I need? Why do those who claim to love me leave me? Who will protect me? Who will hold me?" Speaking for our legitimate dependency needs, our inner children often ask these kinds of questions.

Ignoring Your Inner Child

Imagine you were in the yard when little Jenny was being overwhelmed by the family dog. What would you have done? Most likely, you would have responded as Mel and I did, by protecting and comforting the child. With our own inner children, however, many of us ignore or abuse these "little ones."

John Bradshaw writes, "The most important first step is to help your wounded child grieve its unmet developmental dependency needs . . . . Getting these needs met at the proper time and in the proper sequence is nature's way."[1] Many of us, especially those who feel "there isn't enough," do not provide ourselves with legitimate avenues for getting our developmental needs addressed. And for good reason. As children, we were shamed when we exposed our legitimate needs.

What is your reaction when you see a couple in love? Gazing into each other's eyes, their bodies intertwined, they are unaware that anyone else is on the planet. I can recall many times when I have made critical, shaming remarks about how inappropriate it is for people to "hang on to each other," especially if I was with friends in a public place. Usually I intermixed my ridicule with a dash of humor to get a laugh from those around me. If I honestly examine my reactions, however, I must admit that this hostility is rooted in my own neediness. Seeing people openly expressing their dependency upon each other triggers my inner longings for someone to love and nurture me. I recoil in disgust, hoping no one will see the longing in my eyes.

Shaming others when they expose their legitimate dependency needs is my dysfunctional response to the shame I endured when daring to admit I was needy. Most certainly you have experienced this painful self-punishment as well. In order to enjoy life to its fullest, we must repel these assaults of shame and embrace our inner children with pride, confidence, and determination.

If we succumb to the shame by ignoring or trying to hide our legitimate dependency needs, our inner children become prisoners of our own abuse and neglect. If you do not make certain your needs are met in appropriate ways, "you become an adult with a hurt child inside of you clamoring to get those needs met," Bradshaw explains. "And the child tries to get them met as a child—the only way he knows how. What this amounts to is letting an immature, emotionally starving child run your life."[2]

Many of our addictive behaviors can be traced to our *illegitimately* attending to the *legitimate* needs of our inner children. And this creates one of life's paradoxes—when we ignore our inner children (and all the needs represented therein), we in fact give those parts of ourselves more power, not less. However, the power is unconsciously driven and, therefore, outside of our conscious control. For example, let's say our inner child has a need for comfort, to which we do not respond. Suddenly, we have a craving for chocolate, sex, or alcohol. Others will be driven to work excessive hours or become overly involved with a new lover. If we don't take responsibility for meeting our legitimate needs in legitimate ways, our unconsciouses will push us to meet those needs in illegitimate ways. It is really quite simple. And we each have a choice.

Getting to Know Your Inner Child

What exactly is an inner child? Many in the recovery field speak of "inner-child work," but what does this really involve?

Those of us who have developed an inner child have done so as a defense against childhood abuse and deprivation. One of the psychological defense mechanisms children use to protect themselves is dissociation. In its simplest form, dissociation is self-hypnosis, a way of pretending to be somewhere other than where you actually are. Daydreaming to escape the boredom of an excessively long meeting, for example, is a form of dissociation you may have used recently. Or, perhaps you have allowed your mind to wander while you were driving and, without paying attention to the turns, you arrived at your destination. We all dissociate to one degree or another.

This defense becomes problematic, however, if we used it repeatedly as children as an attempt to escape dangerous situations. Only our minds were able to escape; our bodies were unable to break free of the abuse or neglect. For example, a young girl might try to cope with being sexually assaulted by her mother by pretending she is one of the flowers in the wall paper of her bedroom. She might tell herself that *she* is not being molested. The "other" girl is really the victim. Or a young boy might pretend he is a heroic comic book figure to compensate for his feelings of helplessness while once again watching his father beat his mother. A little girl who is shamed or criticized as being clumsy, might split off that part of herself. Without being aware of doing so, she begins an inner dialogue that echoes her parents' criticism. Later if she stumbles or makes a mistake, she calls herself "stupid" or "ugly."

When, as children, we were unable to truly protect *all* of ourselves from abuse or deprivation, we chose to protect *part* of ourselves. Some separated their minds from their bodies. Others splintered their psyches into sections, like a tree that was hit by lightning. Experts now refer to the inner child and separate inner parts of our personalities as ego states. We may have one or more inner children, each with different ages, for the age we were when we used the defense of dissociation is usually the age of the inner child.

Identifying Your Inner Child

How does an inner child reveal himself or herself? You may catch a glimpse of your inner parts through a variety of ways. These stories are three examples.

Willie didn't like being alone in the house when his wife and children were out. "Why do I feel so anxious? After all, I'm a grown man," he scolded himself. "I should be able to spend a few hours by myself until the family returns." He tried to busy himself fixing a kitchen faucet like he'd promised his wife, but he couldn't concentrate. His mind wandered. The building anxiety began to flood over him. "I can't stand this," he confessed to himself and found he was nearly driven outside. "Maybe I'll just water the lawn." As the water began to spurt from the hose, he remembered watering the lawn when he was a kid. He had liked outside work when he was a boy because it got him out of the house, where all the fighting and yelling was going on. "Yes," he thought to himself, "I like it better out here." In the back of his mind he heard a little boy's sad voice say, "Yes, I like it out here, too."

A curious dream haunted Melinda all morning at work. A young girl had been sitting on her lap. Even though the girl appeared to be around the age of three, there was a strange wisdom in her eyes. The child looked up and said, "I know the secret."

"What secret?" Melinda asked her, but before the girl could respond, Melinda woke up.

Work had been stressful lately, and Zachary had been having those neckaches again. "Maybe a massage would help," he thought earlier and quickly called the masseuse for an evening appointment.

"You have quite a knot here in your neck," the bodyworker said, applying more pressure.

"Ahhhh . . ." Zachary gave a huge sigh and breathed deeply, trying to relax. As the pressure against his muscle continued, an image, frozen in time like a snapshot, suddenly appeared in his mind. It was an image of himself. He was five or six years old and his older brother had him by the neck, pinned against the bed posts. The brother was unzipping Zachary's pants.

"Oh!" Zachary jerked his neck.

"I'm sorry. Did I hurt you?" the body worker asked.

"No, it wasn't you," Zachary sighed sadly. "It wasn't you."

In each of these instances, the inner child, who lives in the unconscious, is breaking through to consciousness, trying to communicate a special message. Each ego state has a story to tell, often forgotten, usually because it is so painful to remember. Inner-child work can be difficult, but it is also rewarding because secrets of the past can finally be faced and the schisms in our psyches can be healed.

Active Imagination

You can use a variety of approaches to communicate with your inner child. The most effective method I have used is active imagination. Developed by Carl Jung, active imagination is the technique of setting up an imaginary conversation with a figure from the unconscious. Robert Johnson writes that active imagination is "similar to dreaming, except that you are fully awake and conscious during the experience. This, in fact, is what gives this technique its distinctive quality. Instead of going into a dream, you go into your imagination while you are awake."[3]

By using your imagination, you can have a conversation with your inner child. Be prepared, however, as your inner child will answer you. Let a friend or your therapist know you are going to begin this type of work so that someone can be available as a support during the process. It's critical that you respect your inner child; he or she knows what you have tried to forget. When you start to talk with your inner child, memories may come back to you that have been repressed for years. Intense emotions, sometimes feeling larger than life, may flood your senses. The intensity of these feelings is often the result of the pain, rage, sadness, or grief that has been bottled up for so long.

The conversation can be conducted in several ways. You may sit quietly, breathing deeply for a few moments and then visualizing your inner child. Imagine what your inner child is wearing, its age, the color of its hair. Begin to ask your inner child questions, such as do you have a special name? What are you feeling? What do you want to tell me?

Another way to use active imagination is to write out the conversation, either in longhand or on the computer. I often use my computer to talk with my inner child. As Robert Johnson recommends, I use lower case for myself and upper case for my inner child. A conversation may look like this:

hi, how are you feeling today?
I AM UNHAPPY BECAUSE YOU HAVE BEEN WORKING SO HARD ON THIS MANUSCRIPT, AND I HAVEN'T HAD ANY TIME TO PLAY.
yes, i've been very busy. i have a deadline to meet.
I WANT TO HAVE SOME FUN. YOU DON'T PAY ANY ATTENTION TO ME ANYMORE.
what would you like to do?
I WANT TO GO SKATING OR TO A MOVIE.
i need to finish this project. i can't go out right now.
YOU ARE JUST LIKE THE OTHER GROWNUPS. NO ONE LISTENS TO ME.
you are right, i have got to make time for you. the headaches are coming back again.

THAT'S ME, YOU KNOW. I'LL GET YOUR ATTENTION ONE WAY OR AN-
OTHER.
so, you are behind the headaches? ok, let's work this out so we can both
get what we need.

Remember, your inner child, like mine, is dedicated to getting your attention one way or another. If we pay attention to
and work cooperatively with our inner parts, we can develop
creative and effective strategies for enjoying life while fulfilling our responsibilities. However, if we ignore parts of ourselves, especially our inner children, they may throw a
tantrum, triggering another addictive episode, coming down
with another virus, or preoccupying our minds so that we are
unable to concentrate.

Open Yourself to Your Inner Child

If you open yourself to your inner child, you will enter a
world long forgotten and waiting for your return. A number
of resources can help you on this journey. I recommend John
Bradshaw's *Home Coming: Reclaiming & Championing
Your Inner Child*, and Robert Johnson's *Inner Work: Using
Dreams & Active Imagination for Personal Growth*. Both of
these books can give you additional assistance in getting to
know your inner child and facilitating healing.

As you open yourself to your inner world, specifically your
inner child, you will most likely face some facts about your
childhood that are difficult and painful. I urge you to trust
your inner child, follow its advice, and be ready to learn. If you
listen, you will finally hear the true story of your childhood,
a truth you must face if you genuinely want to be free to enjoy
the rest of your life.

6

Insist on Safety for You and Your Inner Child

Holding my breath, I watched as the heavily padded self-defense instructor grabbed Connie from behind and roughly threw her to the mat. I winced as her body slapped against the padding. Even though Connie was surrounded by a class of supportive women and she knew that beneath the attacker's hideous mask was Mark, a kind and caring instructor, I could see terror in Connie's eyes. From her vacant, yet frightened look, I could tell she was replaying scenes from the past, the beatings she'd received as a child—there'd been no padded mats to catch her fall then—and the three rapes she had survived when there'd been no practice runs.

Harry, as we referred to Mark when he was wearing his attacker's mask, had climbed on top of Connie, pinning her arms and legs against the mat. She struggled briefly, ineffectively, and went limp. "Use your voice!" we yelled to her from the side lines. Her eyes cleared, focusing for the first time on Harry. "Good," I thought to myself, "she's back in the present, not as a child or a victim, but as a fighter."

"NOOOOOOoooooooo!" A fierce cry filled the room. Connie

glared at Harry. "NOOOOoooooo!" she repeated, as her body filled with massive strength from the depths of her soul, drawing deeply from the power of her rage. Quickly, swiftly, and deftly she used her arms, elbows, legs, and feet to break free from Harry's grip. Turning on her side, she positioned herself with confidence. Harry lunged at her again, but Connie was ready this time. She kicked him with a powerful blow that without the mask would have rendered Mark unconscious. She jumped to her feet, glaring with rage as she looked down at her defeated attacker. In triumph, she ran to join us at the side of the mat as we cheered.

Develop the Skills Needed for Safety

A fearful child cannot play. Since one of the key attributes of play is its ability to absorb our attention, only children who feel safe can abandon themselves to play. Few of us in recovery grew up in households in which we felt safe. To the contrary, we were confronted with danger of all kinds. Some were frightened by loud arguments between their parents, while others feared nightly sexual abuse. Seasons of peace may have been abruptly disrupted by a mother's alcoholic rampage or a father's violent outbursts. Some of us were left, physically or emotionally, to try to navigate an overwhelming and hostile world on our own. Fear and anxiety were constant childhood companions.

Victims of abuse are usually blamed for the hurt they suffer. "You know your father hates your loud music. Why did you set him off by playing that junk so loud? It's your fault he knocked you around." Or maybe the blame sounded like, "If you'd done your chores when I asked you to, you wouldn't have gotten hit." Connie shared with our self-defense class that her mother would hit her and if she started to cry would hit her again for making noise. "I taught myself to endure the pain by pretending to be somewhere else," she explained. "I haven't cried in years. I don't think I know how anymore."

When society blames a child for being abused, the child often internalizes the belief: "I was hurt because I was bad." Most of the children I have worked with, especially the younger ones, are intensely reluctant to hold their parents or other adults responsible for abusive behavior. Instead, I've heard these children say, "I deserved what I got. My mom told me I was a bad seed, just like my dad," or "I am a tramp. Why else would I be molested?"

A child who feels responsible for the abuse may turn that logic around and conclude, "Since I was hurt because I was bad, I can be safe if I am good." Many of the people who come to my workshops have unconsciously associated safety with goodness. Hoping to avoid further pain, these people have invested enormous energy in being *good enough to be safe.*

We know that our brains are able to associate anything together, whether or not these items or experiences actually are related. For example, let's say you visited an amusement park when you were a child, and you wore a yellow shirt. After riding the roller coaster, you became violently ill. You may no longer remember that particular experience, but you now react rather negatively to yellow and the thought of taking your kids to a carnival turns your stomach.

Our brains continually make similar associations. We associate pictures of palm trees with romance and the colors red and green with Christmas. Being near a palm tree does not in any way ensure a romantic interlude, nor does the appearance of two particular colors mean that it is December. Our brains, however, make associations regardless of their accuracy. Most of us associate a wide variety of experiences with feelings or events, few of which accurately reflect the true nature of reality. Even more problematic, however, is that most of these associations are made unconsciously. So unless they draw us into some kind of conflict with the outside world, we are rarely aware of these connections.

Those of us who were blamed for the abuse we experienced as children may have made unconscious associations between being good and being safe. Depending on your family, being good may have meant pleasing adults, over-achieving, keeping family secrets, denying your sexuality, never expressing your true feelings, or cutting off yourself from feeling anything altogether. In an effort to protect yourself from further harm, you dedicated yourself to goodness, only to be abused again . . . and again . . . and again.

The strategy of protecting ourselves by being good doesn't work because there is no actual relationship between goodness and safety. Being good may actually increase the likelihood of your being misused. During years of working in the area of child sexual abuse, I have interviewed a large number of convicted child molesters. One question I have asked these people is, "How do you select your victim?" Repeatedly, I have been told that the molester looks for the good kid or the child who has been taught to obey adults unquestioningly. A child who feels compelled to please adults is more likely to be intimidated into cooperating than a child who is equipped to fight for his or her own safety.

Many of the adults attending my workshops continue to associate being good with being safe. These are the people who say, "Did you hear about Jim? He was such a good man. How could he have died in that car accident?" or "Mary was a saint, always concerned for others. How is it possible that she could get cancer?" These adults are confused because, on an unconscious level, they believe that bad things don't happen to good people. When tragedy does befall a "good" person, they often experience tension, fear, and confusion.

This association is also reflected in logic such as, "I am so angry with myself for parking on the street. Someone broke into my car and stole my radio. If only I hadn't been so stupid, this wouldn't have happened to me." Others say, "Yes, it is terrible that she was raped. But she does dress provocatively, and, after all, she knew the man. In fact, she was out on a date with him. Certainly she should have known what he wanted." As adults, we often blame ourselves and others when we are hurt or violated, and find ourselves in a quandary when our so-called goodness doesn't keep us safe or bring us happiness.

With our inner children as our guides, we can journey back

and listen to the cries, watch the horrors, and endure the losses. But that is not enough. We must look beneath these experiences and uncover the long-term effects of the abuse, the unconscious associations we've made about ourselves, our self-protection, and happiness.

When we make incorrect, and often unconscious, associations between being good and being safe, we rely on ineffective strategies for self-protection. That is what Connie did and she talked about it in our self-defense class. "I actually thought that if I wouldn't cry again, no one would hurt me," she said. "Obviously, that didn't work!"

When we place faith in strategies for being safe that won't keep us safe, we actually place ourselves in further danger by failing to develop the skills genuinely needed for self-protection. Long after the childhood bruises have healed, the sexual offender is behind bars, or the deprivation is forgotten, we continue to carry the faulty unconscious associations we made while we were being abused or deprived. We must discard this lie. Instead of relying on being good as a means of protecting ourselves, we have to learn how to protect our inner children and our adult selves from being revictimized.

Step One: Place Responsibility on the Guilty Party

Instead of blaming the victim, hold the offender responsible. Stop thinking of excuses for why your mother drank excessively or your father beat you with a belt. Give no more explanations for why your teacher fondled you. Stop minimizing the hurt you felt when your dad made fun of your nose or your mom forgot to show up at the awards dinner when you won first place in the speech contest. It is time to place responsibility where it belongs, on the shoulders of the offender.

Once responsibility is placed where it belongs, let go of your false sense of blame. This can be hard to do, because we live in a society bent on blaming the weak for the injustices they endure.

Understanding what makes abusive people tick may help you stop feeling responsible for their actions. Often hurtful people have passive dependent personalities and are so needy themselves that they are unable to view other people as separate beings. As M. Scott Peck writes, "Passive dependent people lack self-discipline. . . . Most important, they lack a sense of responsibility for themselves. They passively look to others, frequently their own children, as the source of their happiness and fulfillment. . . . Consequently they are endlessly angry, because they endlessly feel let down by others who can never in reality fulfill their needs or 'make' them happy."[1]

We cannot make another person happy, no matter how hard we may try. All we can do is take responsibility for ourselves. Passive dependent people, however, try to make others feel responsible for their happiness. It is time to stand up against this pressure, even though doing so may be difficult. With the support of your group, your therapist, and genuine friends, you can discard this distortion and embrace the truth: You are not to blame for the abuse and deprivation you have experienced, no matter what. Remember:

- You are not to blame if your house was robbed, even if you left a back window open or forgot to set the burglar alarm. The only person responsible for the theft is the thief.
- You are not to blame if your spouse hit you in the face, even if you were sassy or yelled or said something that upset your partner. The only person responsible for the hitting is the hitter.
- You are not to blame for being raped, no matter what you were wearing, where you were walking, or how late it may have been. The only person responsible for the rape is the rapist.
- You are not to blame for being ignored as a child, even if you were not as talented as your sister or as athletic as your brother. The only person responsible for the neglect is the parent who neglected you.
- You are not to blame for your parent's drinking, even if you were difficult at times or failed to find out where he or she

hid the bottles. The only person responsible for the alcoholism is the alcoholic.

- You are not to blame for being molested, even if you didn't tell anyone for years or even if it occasionally felt good. The only person responsible for the molestation is the molester.

This list can go on and on. No matter what you did or didn't do, said or didn't say, wore or didn't wear, tried or didn't try, you are not to blame for the abuse or deprivation you have endured. The only person responsible for abuse is the abuser.

Step Two: Acknowledge Danger in the Present

While none of us are to blame for the abuse or deprivation we have experienced in the past, we can learn how to better protect ourselves from being revictimized in the present. The exact measures you need to take depend upon the type of abuse or deprivation you experienced and the current relationship you may have with the offender.

Even if the person or people who hurt you when you were a child are no longer living, then it is still important to examine how your childhood experiences may be affecting your adult behavior and choices. For example, if you still unconsciously link pleasing others to protecting yourself, you may be putting yourself in danger of being revictimized by people with problems similar to those of your childhood abusers. Even though Connie's mother died when Connie was a teenager, her mother was not the last person who hit her. "My first husband would come home drunk and blacken my eyes a couple of times a month," she says. "He would say it was my fault; either I'd burned the dinner or the house wasn't clean enough, you know. Something like that always set him off. I reacted as I did when I was a kid; I'd zone out and never cry."

If you were abused by someone who is still living and still presents a threat to you, it is all the more important to learn new self-protection skills. A rule to remember is *If nothing has changed, then nothing has changed.* Unless those who abused you have undergone extensive therapy, participated on a regular basis in some type of recovery support group or program, or had a radical experience causing him or her to address this passive dependency problem, most likely he or she has not changed. If your mother verbally abused you when you were a child, she probably still calls you the same names or tries the same manipulations with you now. If your father sexually molested you, he is still capable of harming you now, and could be molesting other children such as your little nephew, cousin, or even your own children.

If you fail to act responsibly in the present, facing the past with honesty and courage is not enough. You also must face current danger with an equal measure of honesty and courage. Acknowledge realistic danger, whether it comes in the form of relationship patterns learned in childhood or a present threat from someone who began abusing you years ago.

Step Three: Use Your Anger as Energy for Change

Healthy anger gives us energy and strength far beyond what we can ordinarily muster to overcome dangerous situations. We often feel anger when we have been violated or neglected, and should funnel this powerful emotion into some form of *change.*

While the specific change needed depends on each situation, usually the change required involves protecting yourself in the present and taking measures to prevent another such violation. When you use anger appropriately, the level of anger will equal the amount of energy needed to bring about the proper change.

Imagine the following situation. You are in line at the supermarket, waiting to pay for your groceries. Without looking in your direction, a young man cuts in front of you and, from all appearances, intends to go before you. It is appropriate to feel annoyed by this inconsiderate behavior and his violation of the universally understood rules for standing in line and paying for one's groceries. You could stew over this inconsiderate behavior, letting your annoyance churn in your stomach. Or, you could positively channel the energy generated by your anger into taking care of yourself. You might confront the person, for example, by saying, "Excuse me, but you have cut into the line. Please take your place at the end."

Let's say that this young man had not noticed you for some reason and, after your confrontation, looked embarrassed, apologized, and took his proper place at the end of the line. You can relax and release the anger you felt, knowing that you used it to protect yourself properly.

But for the sake of example, let's say the man turns to you, glares, and then turns back in line, making no move whatsoever. Clearly he knew he was cutting into line and intends to continue with his plan. Now you might feel a stronger sense of anger or violation. You could channel this anger toward yourself, feeling overwhelmed, helpless, or even depressed, or you could use the energy generated from your anger to defend your rightful place. You could turn to the person behind you in line and ask him or her to hold your place. You could then walk around to the checker and loudly explain the situation, asking that the manager be called. The public announcement of this man's misconduct and the potential threat of the manager's arrival could be enough to convince him that cutting in line isn't worth the trouble. He may move to his proper place, perhaps with a few angry words of his own. You could then return to your rightful place in line, having released your anger, and feeling satisfied that you properly cared for yourself.

Now just for the sake of this example, let's imagine that this man was cutting in front of you, not for the more benign reasons cited above, but because he was intending to rob the supermarket. Suppose his position in line was part of his plan, and he had absolutely no intention of moving. By speaking loudly and informing the checker of this man's whereabouts, you unknowingly disrupted his hope of surprising the checker. Suddenly, he grabs you by the arm and pushes you back against the counter. Perhaps stunned at first, you now realize that this man is physically dangerous to you and those around you. You are enraged!

You can use the power of your anger in several ways. If you can get away from the man, you could run screaming for the manager or you could dash for the nearest phone and call the police. If he continued to attack you, and if you are properly trained in self-defense techniques, you could defend yourself physically. Your anger would provide the energy you need to follow through with each strike until he is subdued. In this example, the level of anger increases with the degree of violation. Likewise, the action taken increases in severity.

Not only is it important that we use anger to make changes on our behalf in the present moment, but that we take measures to prevent a similar offense happening in the future. It is unlikely that when you go to the supermarket the following week this same man will cut into the line you happen to be standing in for the purpose once again of robbing the store. There may be little that needs to be done to prevent a recurrence. However, if this particular supermarket is known for an excessive number of robberies, one way to use your anger is to channel the energy into finding another supermarket, even if it means driving further or some other inconvenience.

Using anger to bring about preventive change is most critical when the abuse we suffer comes from people we are in contact with on a regular basis, such as family members, friends, or work contacts. We must take whatever steps are required to protect ourselves. By calling on all the energy we can draw from our rightful anger, we can protect ourselves from repeated abuse. Not only is it important to protect your inner child, but also protect *yourself*, in your physical, spiritual, emotional, and mental entirety.

Step Four: Use Your Anger as Energy to Put Yourself First

I remember my first night in self-defense class. We introduced ourselves and were starting to practice the self-defense moves the instructors had demonstrated. Mark, our padded instructor, was showing us how to deliver a strike to the head. It was my turn to practice, so I nervously walked onto the mat.

"Take your elbow," he instructed, "and strike me in the head." I feebly popped his face mask with my elbow.

"Hit me!" he yelled, so I knocked him harder.

"Carmen!" he bellowed, "hit me hard!"

"But I'm afraid I'll hurt you!" I said, dropping my hands to my side.

Many of us are afraid to make any effort to protect ourselves because we fear that in expressing our own rage we will hurt other people. We have been hurt, and we do not want to be like those who have done damage to us. This fear is valid in that anger is a feeling that can block our ability to empathize with the pain of another person. The ability to empathize is a characteristic of a healthy personality. Generally speaking, it is important to empathize with others so the choices we make take into account the impact on all concerned. However, when we are being attacked or endangered by another person, anger helps us do what needs to be done, put our need for safety first with minimal concern for the abusive person's wellbeing. Out of this misguided fear of hurting someone else, many of us channel our anger away from rather than toward the person or persons who have violated us.

Step Five: Let Your Anger Work for You and Then Let It Go

Anger is a very powerful emotion intended for immediate use. Because anger is so powerful and potentially destructive, it is best expressed and then quickly released from our systems. If we do not use anger immediately and then promptly release it, this intense energy stays with us. Anger does not evaporate like steam. To the contrary, anger, like all emotions, insists on being expressed somehow, someway.

We may have learned too quickly, so quickly that we did not even notice, to turn anger into some self-defeating feeling such as anxiety, depression, self-doubt, resentment, or helplessness. Some of us may store anger within our bodies resulting in painful muscle tension, recurring headaches, ulcers, heart attacks, or even cancer. Others of us have so much anger bot-

tled up inside that the slightest offense sets us off in an outburst far outweighing the current violation.

We can have anger stored up, not only from yesterday when
our supervisor snapped at us, or from last week when a close
friend stood us up for lunch, but also layers and layers retained
from our childhood. For our own health and protection, as well
as for the success of our current relationships, this past anger
must be unearthed, expressed, and released. When we own
our anger and use it for our own benefit, within the appropriate bounds of the present situation, we no longer play the victim or fall prey to becoming an offender. We needn't swing
from one dysfunctional role to another, but can cut a new
course for ourselves, one that is empowered, balanced, strong,
and fair.

Insist on Safety for You and Your Inner Child

Once you have acknowledged the damage of the past and
properly protected yourself in the present, your inner child
will be able to come out of hiding and resume your playtime.
Only children who feel safe are free to play with abandon, fully
connected to their creativity and able to imagine that anything is possible. Learning to enjoy life as an adult is rooted
in our ability to play as children. If you didn't have that chance
when you were a kid, you have a second chance. Once you have
learned how to protect yourself, it is time to play.

7

Accept Responsibility for Your Own Enjoyment

The phone rang and I jumped for the receiver. "Hello?" I asked hopefully, almost desperately.

"Hi, Carmen, it's Angie."

"Oh," I sighed, unable to hide my disappointment.

"Well, thanks a lot," she complained. "It's nice to know you are so glad to hear from me!"

"I'm sorry. Yes, I am glad to hear from you. It's just that I was hoping to hear from Sid this week. He hasn't called," I confessed, "and I feel miserable."

"Well, kid, let's you and me go out tonight and have a good time," Angie suggested enthusiastically. "No reason to sit around waiting for him."

I paused, feeling the energy drain from me. "Thanks for the thought, but I don't really feel like it. I think I need a quiet night at home." Silence. "You know what bothers me the most about him not calling is that I put so much effort into celebrating his promotion. I bought him a great gift and organized a surprise party last weekend. And what do I get out of it? Any sign of appreciation? Does he think about what I may need? No, I get nothing."

Addiction—An Ineffective Enjoyment Strategy

For years I regularly used one specific strategy in an attempt to get my needs met. This strategy was based on the belief that if I were good enough, helpful enough, and giving enough, I would be loved and nurtured in return. Feel free to place this strategy in the ineffective category, and call it addiction.

We all use some strategy in our attempt to get what we need. Some of us are conscious of our strategies, and some of us are not. Codependents, perhaps more than any other addicts, are the most deceived about this dynamic. When in my addiction, I do not recognize that I have any Enjoyment Strategy at all. To the contrary, I see myself as giving rather than taking, as offering to others rather than receiving, as other-focused rather than selfish. But, in fact, I am unconsciously using an ineffective strategy aimed at binding people to me, with the false hope that if they need me, they will love me.

No doubt you have also relied on one or more of the many ineffective Enjoyment Strategies available. Perhaps you tried the "if-I-eat-everything-in-this-refrigerator-in-the-next-hour-and-a-half-I-will-feel-fulfilled" method. Or maybe you used the "if-only-she-would-love-me-everything-in-my-life-would-be-wonderful" approach. At the core of every addiction is the legitimate need to feel safe and to enjoy life. This need just gets twisted around and comes out hurting people, ourselves, and those we claim to love. Our addiction masquerades as an Enjoyment Strategy that promises health, wealth, and happiness, only to deliver sickness, poverty, and pain.

The choice before us is not whether we will have an Enjoyment Strategy, but whether the strategy we use will be dishonest and ineffective or honest and effective.

Making Others Responsible for Our Happiness

Regardless of our addiction of choice, many of us refuse to take responsibility for enjoying our lives. Instead, we use an ineffective Enjoyment Strategy, which is usually indirect, manipulative, and disappointing. Even those of us who have achieved a level of sobriety, as defined by each addiction, can still rely on an Enjoyment Strategy formed in our addictive pasts. Several years into my recovery from codependency I realized that while I was no longer involved in excessive helping activities, I still tended to select one or more people and declare them responsible for my happiness.

When in this dynamic, I may select a particular man I am dating, a special friend, a family member, or a work associate. I then launch into a massive campaign to please, nurture, support, and help this person. Why? Because I care? Some, perhaps. But my real motivation is making the person love me and give me what I want.

If these targeted individuals treat me the way I would like, then I am happy. When the person does not give me what I desire, whether that be attention, affirmation, gifts, or a raise in salary, I am a mess. Getting attended to becomes an obsession, an addiction, and, to no one's surprise, inevitably my efforts result in hurt, disappointment, and even, at times, the demise of the relationship.

Why do we so often try to get our needs met through means that are consistently ineffective and disappointing? Why do many of us relentlessly cling to our ineffective Enjoyment Strategies, even though they fail us time after time? Why do we try to make others responsible for our happiness instead of taking responsibility for ourselves? Here are five reasons why we do not take responsibility for our own happiness: 1) low self-esteem, 2) lack of skill, 3) blaming others for our situation, 4) fear of abandonment, and 5) magical thinking.

1. *Low Self-esteem*

A major reason we don't take responsibility for our own happiness is simple: we feel wrong doing so. Many of us were taught that good children care about others while bad children are selfish. As a child in Sunday school, I learned a song "JOY is spelled *J*esus, *O*thers and *Y*ou." Clearly if I wanted God to love me, I had to put myself last, and attend, instead, to every other human being on the planet. When operating within my addiction, I do not feel that I deserve to spend my money, my time, or my energy on myself. To do so would be selfish. I feel ashamed of acknowledging and addressing my own needs, whether they are needs of dependency, independence, or interdependency. Instead, I feel compelled to deprive myself of what I need and instead give to others.

Have you ever watched a group of toddlers playing? What I love about seeing little ones play is their acute awareness of their own needs and their lack of shame at asserting their own interests. Adults certainly need to be on hand to aid in conflict resolution as these tiny warriors rambunctiously compete for toys, unabashedly enjoy their tasty snacks, and with loud and penetrating voices announce any violation of their rights. We all used to be like that, clear about how we felt and totally shame-free about protecting our territory. While we all need to learn to negotiate and share, I feel rejuvenated when I watch such positive self-esteem in action. It helps me better picture what healthy, childlike self-regard might look like in my own life.

2. *Lack of Skill*

Among the bright faces before me were highly trained, talented, and intelligent people who were good at what they did: therapists, elected officials, teachers, pastors, parents, and physicians. Accustomed to tackling tasks with enthusiasm, anticipating success, these workshop participants were ready for the next workshop exercise.

"I'd like you to get out a piece of paper," I instructed, "and for the next three minutes, write down everything you have done for other people during the past week." Immediately pens were flying across the pages, listing activity after activity.

At the end of three minutes, I gave a second set of instructions. "Now, I'd like you to review your week, and for the next three minutes, write down everything you did to take care of yourself." Looks of confusion came across the crowd. A hand shot up, "What do you mean by the term 'care'?" one person asked. "Could that include a seminar I took on how to become a better parent?" another person inquired. People started to whisper among themselves, hoping for clarification.

"For example," I responded, "did any of you enjoy a visit with a friend during a lunch break?" Again, I faced a sea of blank faces. I realized we had some conceptual problems to face. "Let me try again. How many of you understand the concept 'lunch'?" The crowd broke into laughter, realizing that for many of them, lunch was merely eating a sandwich while working at their desk, not a time for rest or enjoyment. They knew how to work and how to care for others, but when asked to draw on those skills for their own behalf, they drew a blank.

As I tour the country speaking on recovery from codependency, I meet hundreds and hundreds of people who are highly skilled at taking care of other people. Need help? They are there, ready and able to face any emergency. But what about taking care of themselves? Many of us were taught through our families, through school, and perhaps through additional professional or technical training how to care for others. So where are the schools that are ready to teach us how to care for ourselves?

How do we learn the skills necessary for each stage of recovery? What are the best ways for you to meet your legitimate needs? How can you develop and defend proper boundaries, thereby establishing appropriate self-reliance and independence? What skills are needed to create and nurture healthy, balanced relationships with family and friends? How does one become interdependent without getting lost in the relationship? What can we do to get what we legitimately need?

3. Blaming Others for Our Situation

Previously we discussed the importance of holding those persons who have harmed us responsible for the damage they have caused. In order to move toward healing, we must relinquish responsibility for those experiences, abuses, or losses over which we had no control.

However, in my own life and in the lives of many others around me, I repeatedly have seen the tendency to hold others responsible for more than their share. There is an important difference between holding someone responsible for their actions and blaming someone else for the problems in your own life.

When we hold someone responsible for their actions, we can be specific about the offensive behavior, the negative impact, and what steps could be taken to make amends. As discussed previously, only the thief is responsible for the theft, which results in a loss for the person robbed. The thief could make amends by returning the stolen items or, if criminally prosecuted, by being fined or sentenced to jail. Similarly, the physically abusive parent is solely responsible for the assaults which cause physical, emotional, and spiritual damage to the child. The parent could make amends through a variety of ways, such as acknowledging the abuse, paying for medical and psychological treatment the offspring may need, participating in support groups and therapy to deal with the problem, or working the Twelve Steps.

Blaming others for our problems, however, usually means making ill-defined accusations, overstating the negative impact, and providing little avenue for reconciliation. Consider these examples:

> Carl was furious with his father and had been for years. "I hate that man for the way he used to beat my mother," he steamed. "And then he left her here with nothing. I take care of her now, which is a real drain financially. My wife gets upset

with me for all the time I spend over at my mom's place, making repairs and visiting. Plus, it's expensive trying to maintain two households. If my father had been a decent man, my whole life would be different now. My marriage would be better, my mom would be happy, and I'd have the chance to enjoy myself a little instead of running from one place to another taking care of everyone. I truly hate that man."

"If I'd gotten the love I needed as a child," Tanya said as tears came to her eyes, "I wouldn't have this weight problem. After my support groups and therapy, I can see that I overeat to make up for the emotional care I didn't get when I was a kid. Every time I look in the mirror, I think of how different my life could have been if I'd only had a mother who gave me what I needed. Now, I'm alone, overweight, and miserable. It's all her fault."

"I don't know that I'll ever really recover from being molested," Charles said as he held his head in his hands. "I feel so humiliated, so emasculated. I know that's why I have trouble with women today. I don't know, maybe I'm confused about my sexual identity now because of all of this. So much was ruined for me by the molestation. I could be happy today if it hadn't been for the abuse."

In these different examples, we see similar themes common to blame. Each person was legitimately harmed with undeniably negative consequences. In order to heal, each person needed to clearly identify the way in which he or she was victimized by describing the abuse, identifying the abuser, and describing the negative consequences. However, Carl, Tanya, and Charles all made a serious mistake. In the process of honestly confronting their victimizing experiences, they took on the identity of Victim.

One of the most damaging elements of being victimized is being overpowered by someone who does us harm. Not only do we endure the damaging act, we also suffer an additional trauma, losing faith in our own ability to protect ourselves. Recovery from any type of abuse or deprivation is incomplete as long as we retain a sense of helplessness. We take a *passive* stance toward meeting our own legitimate needs. Those of us who perceive ourselves not only as being victimized, but also as being Victims, have not restored our faith in ourselves. Instead, we continue to live as though we were unable to live our current lives to the fullest because of the pain of the past.

I have struggled for years over losses, deprivation, and abuse I experienced as a child from a variety of adults and other children in my life. I have difficulty facing the truth about the extent of the damage I endured. However, I am coming to recognize how easily I get stuck in the pain, seeing myself as a Victim rather than as a competent, talented, and vivacious person who has survived some difficult situations. Making this distinction is critical.

As a Victim I feel powerless, anxious, and furious most of the time. I find myself saying to myself, "If only he hadn't hurt me, my relationships with men would be different today." Or, "There's no hope for me. I'm too weak to overcome this." Sometimes this feeling overwhelms me to the point where I lose faith in my Higher Power and I wonder which is stronger, the power of God to heal and sustain me or the power of dysfunction to maim and defeat me.

When I hold others responsible for what they have done, I am able to define clearly the offense and offer ways amends could be made. But when I am blaming someone, no such clarity exists. I perceive the offense in an exaggerated light, feeling that the impact permeates every facet of my life. Entrenched in my passive dependency, I rarely am clear about how to mend the relationship. Rather, I tend to give mixed, confusing messages, or I throw up my hands in defeated despair, declaring that all is lost.

By blaming others, we give them more power over us than they originally took from us. We not only have to deal with the genuine losses, but also those losses we perpetuate by our self-imposed helplessness. We are unable to play because we are too busy remembering the lost playtimes. We rarely laugh because as Victims we are unable to see anything funny. Life becomes a pervasive sad story as we unconsciously gravitate toward its dark and defeating parts. Unable to be spontaneous, we are rigid and worried about the next abusive episode. We fall asleep at night counting our losses, not our blessings.

Perhaps the most damaging aspect of taking on the role of Victim is the rage we generate, which is rarely channeled in helpful ways. We fume, we fret, we regale tale after tale of the ways we have been hurt. We store anger in our bodies and make ourselves sick rather than channel it for self-protection. Instead of viewing our relationships as opportunities for intimacy, fun, and pleasure, we weight them down with our pain, rage, and losses. We want them to make up for what we didn't get before, but they can't do that.

4. Fear of Abandonment

The workshop divided into several small groups to discuss how to bring more enjoyment and fun into their lives. As I walked around the room responding to individual questions, one woman motioned to me. "To me," she said, "taking responsibility for my own happiness means giving up any hope I have for being nurtured or having fun. If I don't believe that my husband, my kids, or my friends can make me happy, then what else do I have? I see myself being all alone, trying to give myself something I don't have to begin with." The group nodded, adding support to this sentiment, as if they all feared this lonely, hopeless state.

This fear is based on a misunderstanding of what taking responsibility for yourself actually means. To those raised in dysfunctional homes, it means being abandoned. It means being left all alone to navigate by yourself, because no one else is capable or interested in helping you. To those of us who have embraced the Perspective of Scarcity, taking responsibility for ourselves means a perverted form of independence, not based in positive self-regard and a sense that others are supportive and available, but based in desperation, deprivation, and disappointment.

Convinced there isn't enough, many of us view our own needs as being too profound to address and our desires too powerful to manage. We look outside ourselves hoping someone else is strong enough and caring enough to do what we feel is beyond us. Taking responsibility for ourselves can feel like another agonizing experience of deprivation. As the woman in the seminar told me, "If I let go of my hope that someone else can nurture me, then I have nothing left but my agonizing loneliness."

5. *Magical Thinking*

A primary reason we have difficulty taking responsibility for our own lives is that many of us engage in magical thinking.

"If you give, you will receive."

That is what I was told. Since I wanted to receive, I started to give. I didn't give because I wanted to give. I gave for the specific purpose of receiving. The problem with this formula is that it doesn't work. I gave, and gave, and gave some more, but didn't receive anything. What little I had I gave away, and I had less than before. Magical thinking is manipulative thinking, and it underlies most addictive processes.

When we have a healthy spirituality and a sound relationship with God, when we have a community of balanced relationships, and we then give to others, we receive in return. We receive, not because we give, but because we are surrounded by people who love us and who, by their own choice, nurture us. But dysfunctional systems, whether spiritual, emotional, or relational, contain no give and take, no fairness or concern for all parties involved. Whatever you offer will be taken, and nothing will be offered in return.

If we seek any one primary source of pain and confusion for many of us who feel deprived and lonely, its roots are in this form of magical thinking. We believe, to our core, that we will be rewarded for our addictive efforts. We will not. I guarantee everything you do that is consciously or unconsciously rooted in magical thinking will be a colossal disappointment.

What forms does magical thinking take?

Perhaps you are a parent who is over-invested in your children. If you make your children responsible for your happiness, without a doubt, you will have your heart broken. Children grow up and leave home, and leave you. Do you tell yourself that even though your boss has ignored your repeated efforts to impress him, if you just work harder, put in extra hours, you will finally get the recognition you need? Don't count on it. Are you daydreaming creative ways to make yourself indispensable to the woman you love, hoping she will finally fall in love with you and give you the attention you feel you deserve? She won't. She'll take what you give her and, then, probably fall in love with a guy you think treats her poorly.

Where is the justice in all of this? Wherever it is, it isn't here.

Making Others Responsible for Our Happiness

If I am unable, unwilling, or too fearful to take responsibility for myself, I naturally will rely on others. Since these poor souls rarely volunteer for this job, and often have no ability or intention of being my source of happiness, they are victims of my addiction.

Unaware of what I am doing, I place an unrealistic responsibility on their shoulders. No one can make someone else happy, though many of us have tried to be superhuman for another person. I take on the role of passive dependent, using others in the same way that I was used, thereby passing on the Perspective of Scarcity.

I set these people up to become addicted to me. As a codependent, I have tried to give all I had to the care of others, feeling that I alone was responsible to help those in my life. I have felt both the weight of responsibility and the thrill of believing that someone needed me. When I make someone responsible for my happiness, I set them up to play that same role in my life, to be my codependent. I make them feel indispensable and excessively important. In fact, I make addiction a requirement of our relationship.

Oddly, I claim to care for these people. I may tell a friend or significant other, "I love you so much, which is why I need to talk with you every day." I may respect my supervisor so much that I feel devastated if she does not affirm my work. But underneath, I am back in the grip of my need to control. This is another way I victimize those I make responsible for my happiness. I pour my energy into trying to make them make me happy. I scheme, I whine, perhaps I withdraw and then show up with gifts, all to get someone else to put energy into making me happy. When caught in this dynamic, however, I refuse to put energy *directly* into my own happiness. I adamantly insist on the indirect route.

It is an odd dance, this addictive two-step. I view myself as a giving, loving person who nurtures and cares for others. But when I feel a need for nurturance, I feel left out, overlooked and underpaid. I step to the beat of this seductive music, only to find I am the only one on the dance floor. As a codependent, I have invested my money, my time, and my creativity in the misguided care of someone else, even to the point of damaging my health, spiritual growth, and peace of mind. I have been willing to take responsibility for everyone *except* myself. Why? Because I was a noble humanitarian? I wish. No, unconsciously, and maybe a little consciously, I thought that if I were a good person, a giving person, a helpful person, I would be loved. However, every time I use my caring as a form of manipulation or as a means to getting what I need, I am always disappointed.

Accepting Responsibility for Our Passion for Living

Here are five initial steps you can take toward accepting responsibility for your own enjoyment of life.

1. Invest Energy in Increasing Your Self-esteem

When I was a little girl, I loved to climb a large tree in our backyard. One afternoon, I lost my balance and wedged my arm between two of the branches. Even though my parents rushed me to the doctor and I received immediate medical care, my elbow was permanently damaged and to this day I cannot fully extend my right arm. I grew up feeling self-conscious about my injury.

Being unable to lock my elbow, I found participating in many sports difficult. I felt I couldn't participate in certain gymnastic activities like tumbling or the parallel bars. My muscles tire easily, so excelling at games requiring extensive upper body strength and coordination like basketball and tennis didn't seem to be an option for me. This once active little girl became a self-conscious, non-athletic woman.

In hopes of increasing my self-esteem, particularly about my body, I recently took a risk. With the support of a dear friend who promised to stay close by and to go at my pace, I signed up for a skiing lesson. Self-conscious and frightened, I slowly learned to snow plow. Several times I felt over-whelmed, and I voiced my desire to give up before the lesson was through. My friend, however, patiently encouraged me to stay to the end. And I am so glad she did!

By the end of the day, I was actually skiing down the mountain, not fast, mind you, but skiing. Since this sport depends primarily on lower body strength, I was able to recapture the exhilaration of feeling athletic again, that love for activity I knew so well as a child. I now consider myself a skier, not an expert skier, but a skier nevertheless. This activity has redefined how I feel about myself and definitely helped raise my self-esteem. My inner child once loved her body and the joy of athletic activity. Now, by parenting my inner child, I have recaptured what was lost.

A natural outcome of properly parenting your inner child is an increase of self-esteem. It is critical that you overcome the shaming messages you receive from others, and sometimes from yourself when you address your own needs. As you acknowledge and attend to the legitimate needs of your inner child, you simultaneously communicate to yourself a deeper regard for your perceptions, desires, and worth.

In addition, it is important to consciously attend to those areas that are particularly debilitating to you. How were you criticized as a child? What enjoyable activities do you deny yourself because you feel self-conscious? Would you benefit from special training or tutoring in an area to increase your sense of mastery? Have you always wanted to paint or dance or sing or act, but felt too self-conscious to try? Accepting responsibility for your happiness will require that you attend to your own self-care and nurturance.

2. Increase Your Enjoyment Skills

Many of us rely on others to care for us, not out of intentional design but out of default. We simply do not know how to care for ourselves. We might be willing, but are unaware that self-care requires the development of specific skills, not unlike the skills needed in our work. If work skills require years of education and practice, then self-care skills also require the mastery of a body of knowledge and a specific set of activities. These skills can also be learned and mastered.

Many of us rely repeatedly on one ineffective strategy, confusing our method with the goal. For example, you might say to yourself, "If only she would love me, my life would work out," or "If my son would get a job and straighten up, everything would be wonderful," or "Why can't I get that promotion I deserve? I would have everything I need."

These statements are strategies, not end goals. Look underneath these statements. What do you *really* want? Perhaps you have a legitimate need for love and intimacy. Or maybe you need appreciation and a sense of accomplishment. Perhaps a need for security and a sense of mastery drives you. To get what you want, you must first know what you want and then create the strategy.

Let's say you look beneath your strategy and discover a need for a deeper experience of love in your life. You are investing a great deal of energy into a particular relationship that is not producing the outcome you desire. The person you have selected, the person you may even claim to love, is the *means* to your goal, not the goal itself. You may easily become more connected to the strategy you've devised than to your genuine need.

The tendency to confuse the means with the goal holds true for any strategy you may be using, whether the focus is on relationships such as lovers, children, or co-workers or accomplishments such as financial gain, career advancement, weight loss or any other personal objective. When you become more bonded to your strategy than to your legitimate needs, your strategy immediately becomes an ineffective one. You get the cart before the horse.

To develop an *effective* Enjoyment Strategy, you must first clearly define your legitimate need. Some people realize they need to address legitimate dependency needs for nurture, security, or attention. Others find they have needs for space, boundaries, or independence. Still others discover needs for intimacy and interdependency.

Once your needs are accurately identified, you can then develop a variety of approaches to meet those needs, not just one compulsive pattern that disappoints and frustrates you. Rather than depend on one addictive pattern (and usually one or two over-taxed friends), I devise a plan that includes a variety of people, experiences, and approaches. As a consequence, I experience more nourishment and less deprivation. As more nurturance comes into my life from a variety of sources, I feel less desperate, less grabby, and less needy. Since I am being less demanding, my friends are more relaxed and open with me. When I do ask for attention from others, they are often more willing and able to respond. The cycle becomes one of accumulating more and more abundance as my legitimate needs are met.

As I have accepted responsibility for my own life, for my own inner child, my self-esteem, my thought patterns, and my skill development, my lifestyle has changed radically. I rely less on the approval of others, and I am better able to determine what fits for me. More importantly, I am more deeply rooted in my own passion for living, more able to enjoy each day with enthusiasm and positive anticipation.

3. *Relinquish Your Role as Victim*

Letting go of our roles as Victims can be difficult. For many of us in recovery, the label is our new basis of identity. There are many who criticize the recovery movement because it seems to label people as forever "diseased." Some branches of the recovery movement insist that we will be addicts our entire lives, no matter what we do, and we can never expect any significant changes. In what I believe to be a sincere effort to give people hope by declaring addiction a disease, as opposed to a moral sin or evidence of a lack of will, the recovery movement has communicated to some that healing is impossible.

In contrast, some people, in religious circles as well as secular, promote "quick fix" answers to extremely complicated problems. Some religious groups claim that through faith in God, anyone can be healed of any malady, emotional, spiritual, or physical. Secular groups declare that positive thoughts or repeating affirmations will resolve any number of wounds buried in the unconscious.

What is the truth here? Is recovery simple or complex? Easy or hard? A matter of the will or an endless trail of Twelve Step meetings? Are we forever damaged or is genuine healing possible? Once you've been abused as a kid, can you never be free of the scars?

To these competing questions, my answer is, well . . . yes and no. Every person must decide how to deal with pain and how to get what he or she needs. There is no escaping these tasks. Genetic factors inherited at birth and unique childhood experiences have defined our unconscious minds and have molded them toward selecting specific strategies. Some people are more prone to choose to avoid pain rather than embrace and learn from this inevitable part of life. Others may be inclined to rely on others rather than accept responsibility for their own joy in life.

Our genetic makeup is unchangeable. So is the past. If you were molested as a child, that will always be true. If you were physically assaulted, no mind game will alter that reality. If

you used alcohol to numb your pain, you will always be suscep-
tible to that form of self-destruction. We cannot change the
past. We can, however, change the *meaning* of the past.

Several years ago I was assaulted. Even though I was a
mental health professional and an expert on victimization issues, I responded like many victims. First, I pretended it
didn't happen, then I wondered if I weren't somehow responsible, and finally, for several years, I felt fearful and unsafe no
matter where I might be.

I blamed this experience for problems I was having in my
relationships. When men became confrontive or aggressive, I
would nearly faint in fear. No longer confident in my own abilities to fight back, I became excessively compliant with men
or women whom I felt might overpower me. Without consciously choosing to, I took on the identity of Victim.

Finally, last year I decided to turn that horror into something else, anything else. One way I chose to change the meaning of my experience was by taking a self-defense class.
Through the various scenarios we enacted, I emotionally re-
lived my victimizing experience. I remember the night that I
relinquished my identify as Victim and redefined myself as
fighter.

Because of the assault, my life has been forever changed.
Nothing can erase that night from my past, nor can I somehow
declare myself unaffected. I am a different person, a different
woman, because of that experience. But the assault no longer
defines *who* I am. I have taken that power back into my own
hands. I have chosen how to define myself.

I used to think back on the assault and feel powerless and
ashamed. Now, it reminds me of my courage and fills me with
a sense of healthy pride. Before I redefined myself, when I
drove by that part of town, I'd feel frightened and tearful. But
I am no longer afraid. I am convinced that given those same
circumstances, I would not respond as a powerless, disoriented victim but as a trained and powerful opponent. I realize
if attacked again, I may get hurt, but not in the same way I
was hurt before. I also know that my attacker will not walk

away without a scratch. Now that I have learned these valuable lessons in self-defense, and more importantly, now that I know how to trust myself when faced with danger, I will never be hurt that same way again.

The physical wounds of that attack healed quickly. The emotional wounds lasted for years. I became a Victim and focused my energy on blaming my assailant. In a misguided effort to protect myself, I closed my heart. As Susan Jeffers writes, "A closed heart helps us deny our shadow, our dark side, as Carl Jung called it. While we attribute greed, ugliness, and aggression to the enemy, we cannot see it within ourselves. And just as importantly, when we blind ourselves to the beauty in others, we can't see the beauty within ourselves. While we might feel superior, we certainly don't feel good about who we are and how we are behaving. Thus, totally cut off from our essence, it is no wonder that we are confused about who we are and what we should be doing for the rest of our lives."[1]

If you find yourself in this situation, I recommend these books: *The Courage to Heal,* by Ellen Bass and Laura Davis, and *Forgive & Forget,* by Lewis B. Smedes. Both have excellent material on forgiveness. While we should hold those who hurt us accountable for the damage done, we only hurt ourselves when we hold on to blame. An important element of forgiveness is giving up what we will never get from those who hurt us. Some of us may want an apology. Others may want revenge. Rarely, if ever, do we get what we want from those who caused the damage. Until we are able to release false expectations, we are still under the influence of fear and unable to enjoy the passion of play, still connected to past pain and unopen to pleasure.

"If you cannot free people from their wrongs and see them as the needy people they are," Smedes asserts, "you enslave yourself to your own painful past, and by fastening yourself to the past, you let your hate become your future."[2]

"There comes a time," Bass and Davis write, "when what you feel about the abuser is less important than what you feel about yourself, your current life, and your future. The abuser is not your primary concern. You say, 'I am my primary concern. Whether the abuser rots or not, I'm going on with my own life.' You recognize that many of your current problems stem from past abuse, but you also recognize that you have the power to make satisfying changes."[3]

One of those satisfying changes is taking responsibility for your own enjoyment so that you can finally feel safe enough to play.

4. *Learn to Parent Your Inner Child*

Like many lessons I have learned through my recovery journey, this one is paradoxical. As I accept responsibility for my own happiness, I find I am more connected to nurturing people, not less. As I relinquish my unrealistic expectations that others will somehow make up for what I didn't get as a child, I experience more healing than I dreamed possible. How does this happen?

First, I had to face my own passive dependency. Because I did not receive what I needed as a child, I became passively dependent on the care of others. As long as I try to meet those legitimate needs in illegitimate ways, I always will experience life as containing not enough. It is true, there isn't enough for me if I approach others from a Perspective of Scarcity.

However, if I view these needs for care and nurturance as legitimate concerns of my inner child, I can assume responsibility for properly parenting her. When I assume responsibility for my own inner child, I no longer look to others for what she needs. I, as inner parent, take on that responsibility.

Accepting this responsibility reframes how I approach my feelings of fear, anger, sadness, and disappointment as well as my needs for play, comfort, laughter, and excitement. While I may include others in this process, I no longer *expect* others to care for me. I look for ways to care for myself, the same way I would care for my child. For example, rather than feeling deprived of nurturance through touch, I now take the responsibility for receiving weekly professional massages. While a professional massage does not replace or eradicate the unique nurturance provided through the caress of a lover, the massage does nurture me, physically, emotionally, and spiritually in a way that makes me feel *less needy*.

Instead of relying solely on my friends to help me sort out my problems, I now take responsibility for seeing a therapist regularly. Depending on the amount of support I need, I may see my therapist once, twice, or three times a week. While paying a therapist to meet with me does not replace the unique support possible through friendship, receiving this form of professional support nurtures me and makes me feel *less needy*.

While I used to feel depleted from my work and wonder why God wasn't sorting everything out for me, I now regularly schedule weekend spiritual retreats where I rest and reflect on the nature of my spiritual life. I can't say that at the end of these weekend getaways I have discovered all truth or uncovered the ultimate answers to the meaning of life, but taking responsibility for planning these times has deepened my spiritual walk and, again, made me feel *less needy*.

I still need my friends and family. Receiving positive feedback from colleagues is important to me, but not to the same extent that I once needed it. I once craved affirmation and support like a little child, overwhelmed by a big and scary world. As I take responsibility for my inner child and address her legitimate childlike needs, I am better able to approach my exterior support system with my legitimate adult needs.

5. *Adopt Abundance Thinking*

Magical thinking must be replaced by abundance thinking. It is critical that you identify your magical thoughts and replace them with statements about how the world really works.

Oddly enough, abundance thinking is also paradoxical. While I no longer use the idea that "if I give I will receive," as a manipulation, I do believe that "if I give up, I will receive." I have found that when I give up trying to manipulate others and focus instead on addressing my own needs, I am more likely to receive what I desire. When I cease trying to make my friends give me what I need, at times they have surprised me by nurturing me in wonderful ways I never expected. If I give up giving as a form of manipulation and instead give to others out of a clear expression of my caring, often people spontaneously give back out of genuine gratitude.

I have seen this in the lives of others as well. I've seen parents throw up their hands in despair, finally giving up on their children, only to discover a deeper, more authentic relationship developing among all family members. I've watched colleagues, worn out and disappointed, give up trying to please their bosses and concentrate instead on taking pride in their work. Then, to their amazement, they discover promotions or new job opportunities awaiting them. I've watched friends run themselves ragged, desperately trying to earn love until one day they snap, no longer willing to play the doormat. As they give up and walk away, interestingly enough, their love interests suddenly seem more interested in them.

Is this a magical formula? Am I proposing that you now use this approach as a new method of controlling or manipulating others? No, not at all. In fact, if you turn giving up into another form of magical thinking, those you are trying to control will continue to thwart your schemes. Abundance thinking has no gimmicks and no guarantees. For us to accept responsibility for ourselves we have to genuinely give up our attempts to control others. We must cease taking responsibility for the well-being of others, with no promises. Don't expect magic, but be on the lookout for a few miracles. Without a doubt, miracles will be headed your way.

8

Discover Your Own Enjoyment Style

I often ask participants in my seminars to create a fantasy list of every experience they think may be nurturing or fun. Usually people smile at each other and self-conscious giggles erupt across the room. A few heads drop immediately as pencils scribble madly across papers. Most sit for a moment and stare into space, completely at a loss. I usually allow only three minutes for this exercise because, sadly enough, most people run out of ideas in a short time.

While many of us are willing to have fun, most do not know how to have fun. Many of us are unaware of what we like or don't like, what nurtures us or tires us, what makes us laugh or drags us down. Do you know how you best receive nurturance? Do you know what makes you feel refreshed and renewed? Are you able to determine which experiences will prove pleasurable and which will be disappointing? You must learn more about yourself so you can develop the most effective Enjoyment Strategy possible.

Three Styles of Enjoying Life

"I love going to the beach!" Sylvia exclaimed, as I parked the car.

"Just look at how deep blue the water is!" Carolyn sighed, as the three of us climbed out of the car. I waved to the sea gulls boisterously squawking overhead.

Sylvia smiled, tossing a piece of bread to the gulls from a large basket she had packed for our lunches. I reached for the tape player and my favorite cassette tapes. Carolyn was already snapping pictures of the blue vista with her new camera. "I can't wait to see how these shots turn out," she grinned.

"Don't you just love the feel of sand between your toes?" Sylvia giggled as we trekked across the bluff. Carolyn pointed toward the cliffs, "Hey, let's sit up there on the ridge. I'll bet the view is great from up there."

"Oh, come on, Carolyn," Sylvia protested. "I want to be closer to the water." Waving her snorkel, she said, "I can't wait to dive into that surf."

"Whatever we do, let's stay away from those kids over there," I said pointing to a group of teenagers up near the cliffs with their radio blasting. "I want to be able to hear myself think! Not to mention this new tape I've been waiting to hear."

Clearly outvoted, Carolyn trudged after us toward the water's edge. After placing our towels on the sand, Sylvia opened the basket and asked if we wanted anything to eat. "No thanks," Carolyn responded. "I think I'll head to the cliffs and take some more pictures."

"You're not going swimming?" Sylvia asked, in amazement.

"No, I don't really like getting wet and sandy," Carolyn responded. Scanning the horizon, she smiled broadly. "Ah, how I love the beach. It is so beautiful here."

I joined her in rapt appreciation. "I know what you mean. There's nothing so peaceful as listening to the rhythm of the waves."

"Well, you two can waste your time sitting here all day if

you'd like," Sylvia declared, jumping to her feet. "I'm going in the water!" she called as she ran toward the waves.

Carolyn, Sylvia, and I all thoroughly enjoyed our day at the beach, but because we have different Enjoyment Styles, *what* we enjoy and *how* we enjoy the beach differ greatly. Carolyn has a Visual Enjoyment Style and experiences the beach primarily through her sense of sight. For a visual person, going to the beach means scanning the changing colors of the sky as the sun sets beneath the dark blue horizon or watching the gray and black sea birds scurry across the sand digging for crabs.

In contrast, Sylvia primarily enjoys her world through kinesthetic or body experiences. Since Sylvia has a Body Enjoyment Style, going to the beach means splashing in the water, digging her hands deep into the sand hunting for crabs, and stretching out to feel her skin being warmed by the sun.

As someone with an Auditory Enjoyment Style, I receive my pleasure primarily through my sense of hearing. The beach nurtures me through the comforting rhythm of the waves pounding against the sand, the familiar calls of the sea birds, and the whistling of the wind across the dunes at sundown.

While each person has the capacity to enjoy life in all three of these avenues, most of us have one dominant Enjoyment Style. How do we discover our primary Enjoyment Style? Our Enjoyment Styles give three clues: 1) the kinds of words we use, 2) how our eyes move as we think and talk, and 3) our behavior patterns, tastes, and preferences.

Clue #1—The Words We Use

Since each Enjoyment Style experiences life differently, the words each type of person uses to describe experiences also differ. Let's say you were asked to describe your winter vacation. If you are a visual person, you will have a tendency to describe how your vacation *looked*, perhaps using words such as bright, colorful, dark, clear, or vague. For example, you might say, "The view from the chalet was postcard perfect, with the snow white and glistening as far as the eye could see."

If you have a Body Enjoyment Style, however, you would be more likely to describe how your vacation *felt*, using words such as cold, soft, harsh, tasty, or dry. You might describe your experience this way, "A cold wind blew up in the late afternoon. It was hard to ski because the snow iced up in patches, making it extremely slippery. It sure felt good that night to get back into the chalet, where we warmed up by the fire and sipped hot cider."

We audio folks enjoy our world primarily through the sense of hearing. If you have an Auditory Enjoyment Style, you would probably describe how your vacation *sounded*, using words such as quiet, harmonious, musical, thundering, or hissing. In describing your winter vacation you might say, "What struck me most was how quiet it is on the slopes with the snow dampening every sound. As I rode up the ski lift, all I heard was the faint squeaking of the gears against the cables and the swishing of the skiers below. Once I was at the top, everything was so quiet, all I could hear was my heart pounding with excitement."

What impressed you most about your last vacation? (You have taken a vacation in the last decade, haven't you?) Was it the vivid sunset? The clear blue skies? The smiles on the faces of your children? Maybe you have a Visual Enjoyment Style.

Or, do you most remember the comforting rhythm of the train as it chugged through the mountain passes? The taste of the local cuisine? The warmth of your partner by your side? If you are most connected to the bodily sensations, you may have a Body Enjoyment Style.

Perhaps, like me, you remember the calypso music as it floated over the lagoon or the engaging laughter of your travel companions. Did the lapping of the water against the side of the house boat lull you to sleep? Are songs you sang in the car still ringing in your ears? Maybe you have an Auditory Enjoyment Style.

Clue #2—Eye Movement

When we converse with another person, we alternatingly look into his or her eyes and then look away. *Where* we look when we look away provides us with another clue about our Enjoyment Style.

If you have a Visual Enjoyment Style, your eyes may move up to the right or up to the left, as you look up to remember your experience. Most people with a visual enjoyment style have a pattern of upward eye movements when they are engaged in conversation. Those with a Body Enjoyment Style tend to glance down to either side, as if to check their bodies' experience at any given moment. Those of us with Auditory Enjoyment Styles tend to look off to the side, toward our ears, as if to remember how an experience sounded to us.

Since it's impossible to observe your own eye movements, enlist the assistance of a friend. Ask your friend to carry on a conversation with you, asking open ended questions such as "describe your home, your childhood, your car," or any event, item, or experience that may bring you pleasure. At first you will probably be self-conscious about your eye movement and your gaze will wander. But once you become more absorbed in the conversation, you naturally will look your friend in the eye and then look away, in a regular patterned direction, either upward, downward, or sideways.

Instruct your friend to avoid asking you leading questions such as, "describe how your home *looks*," or "how did it *feel* to be a child," or "describe the *sound* of your car's engine." Regardless of our primary Enjoyment Style, all of us are able to relate in all three styles. When asked specifically how something looks, we all can respond in visual terms and will instinctively look upward as we speak. Similarly, when asked to describe sounds, we all are able to do so, and will naturally look to the side while responding. Our eyes will drop to one side or the other, when asked to describe how a particular experience felt to us. To determine your particular preference, the questions must be phrased so that any of the three styles could respond.

One of the most revealing questions you can be asked is to describe an experience in which you were loved. A visual person may say, "I knew he loved me when he showed up at my door with flowers and gazed deeply into my eyes." If you have a body enjoyment style, you might respond, "When she wrapped her arms around me and held me close, that's when I knew how she felt." Or the auditory person may say, "I heard it in his voice, the way he said 'I love you.' I knew then that he really cared."

Clue #3—Behavior and Preferences

For years, I was confused by the difficulty a couple of my friends and I had each time we tried to agree upon a restaurant. We all seemed to have strong preferences, usually different, with little understanding of why a particular restaurant would be at all appealing to the others. Now, however, that my friend and I have identified our Enjoyment Styles, our preferences are more easily understandable, though only now we negotiate with passion and intensity for our beloved styles.

Being auditory, I place a high priority on how the restaurant sounds. If I am in a loud and feisty mood, I prefer to go where the music is booming and the energy is high. On the other hand, if I desire intimate conversation, I want to be in a quiet environment, with space and privacy.

Tod, with a Visual Enjoyment Style, is naturally drawn toward restaurants by how they look. The decor with the ambiance, the colors, and the lighting is the essential element influencing his choice.

Fran, with a Body Enjoyment Style, asserts strongly that a restaurant should be chosen for how it feels, which includes the comfort of the chairs, the time waiting to be seated, and, perhaps most importantly, the quality of the food. How a place looks or its noise level has low priority on Fran's list.

It is easy to see how our Enjoyment Styles can come into conflict. I want a quiet evening. Tod, however, may want to try out a trendy new club which has great decor but no carpeting and crowded tables. "Too loud for me," I lament. Fran complains about the hard chairs and questionable quality of cuisine.

Preferences and tastes vary according to one's Enjoyment Style. For example, a visual person is more likely to live in a home that is nicely decorated and neatly kept. If you have a Visual Enjoyment Style, you tend to take special care of your appearance and have a cultivated eye for style. You may find it difficult to enjoy yourself in situations you consider messy, ugly, unkempt, or unsightly.

On the other hand, an auditory person is likely to live in a quiet environment, probably equipped with a good stereo system and a wide array of musical selections. We audio folks may love to talk and consequently run up an amazingly large phone bill. If you have an Auditory Enjoyment Style, you may be unable to have a good time in a place that is too noisy, too quiet, that lacks adequate musical nurturance, or that limits your ability to converse.

The body person likely lives in a physically comfortable home, with soft couches and chairs and a practical decor. If you have a Body Enjoyment Style, you are more likely than the others to have your refrigerator stocked with tasty delights. When at home, you may lounge around in old, comfortable slippers and a soft robe, undaunted by its ragged appearance. It's comfortable, and that's what matters to you. You may find it difficult to relax in situations that do not cater to your physical comfort. Body and auditory people seem less concerned with the way things look, as long as they feel or sound attractive.

Discover Your Enjoyment Style

As I have stressed before, I believe that pleasure, passion, and nurturance are available to all of us, every day. One reason many of us feel deprived is simply because we are unaware of how we best experience happiness, joy, excitement, and pleasure. We miss opportunities for pleasure and nurturance that are available to us every day, merely out of ignorance of how we could cooperate with our style. Unclear as to how to best enjoy ourselves, we can find ourselves being pressured to enjoy a given experience the way one of our friends may enjoy life, even though that person's style may be quite different from our own.

If you are going to embrace fully a passion for living, enjoying the nurturance that is available to you, you must know yourself well enough to understand how you enjoy life. I urge you to study your Enjoyment Style. You are worth the effort. Ask a friend to interview you, asking open-ended questions and then observing the kinds of words you use and the pattern of your eye movements. Pay attention to yourself, watching for the times when you experience the most joy and pleasure. Knowing your Enjoyment Style can be one of the most effective keys you can discover to unlock your ability to enjoy life.

9

Explore New Ways to Play with Your Inner Child

"This is ridiculous, Carmen!" Alan grinned as he clung to the side of the skating rink. "How did you ever talk me, a grown man, into going skating?"

Skating up beside him, I laughed, "I didn't talk you into this, your inner child did!"

Wobbling out onto the floor, Alan smiled, "Yeah, I always wanted to skate when I was a kid, and never got to." At the end of the day Alan had a few bruises on his knees, but some of the wounds in his heart had started to heal.

The Paradox of Play

Play is one of life's many paradoxes. Play, by definition, is an activity that engages our attention solely by the delight of participation. There is no goal to be met other than the pleasure play gives us. And yet, as we previously discovered, play has many significant benefits, without which our childhood development may be seriously impaired.

The areas of development that may need healing in your life

can be addressed through learning how to play with your inner child. This type of play is different from forms of adult play I will address in the next chapter. The purpose of this type of activity is to give you a second chance at play experiences you didn't receive as a child, thereby healing areas that may have been damaged, and to allow you to learn how to engage in an activity for its sheer enjoyment.

Obstacles to Playing with Our Inner Child

1. Feeling Silly

As with Alan, actually getting involved with a play activity, especially those that are usually reserved for young children, may trigger feelings of shame or embarrassment. Playing may feel odd at first. You may feel a little self-conscious, or even foolish.

If you have ever watched children at play, you may have noticed how carefree and comfortable they seem, engrossed in their activity, not in self-conscious observation. Your discomfort may arise not only from the more obvious self-conscious concerns of being an adult doing something childish, but also from triggering old feelings of shame you experienced as a child when your playtime was disrupted.

I deal with my feelings of embarrassment regarding playtime with my inner child in two ways. First, I sometimes play by myself. For example, I may paint a picture or play with clay. I imagine myself playing with my inner child, and do so privately.

I also deal with this discomfort by involving someone I trust a great deal. Alan, a long-time friend, knew that I would not make fun of him or undermine the importance of his inner child work. I was more than happy to go skating with him and his inner child, as I would have been willing to join a friend taking a son or daughter on an outing. When we have play experiences that can be shared without blame or shame, a great deal of healing takes place.

2. Not Knowing How to Play

A second obstacle to playing with your inner child is more practical. Many of us just don't know how to play. This is where your inner child can be very helpful. By using visualization or active imagination, you can talk with your inner child and allow him or her to teach you how to play. Children love to create, imagine, and explore. Allow your inner child to speak freely. Listen carefully to the way you respond to your inner child. You may find that as a learned response from childhood, you immediately put down, minimize, or underrate the creative ideas of your inner child.

If your inner child wants to fly kites, resist the urge to say, "Oh, it's too cold to go out today," or "I'd feel stupid flying a kite." Grab a jacket and a ball of string and head for the park.

Or, maybe your inner child wants to climb a tree or play with jacks or cuddle a stuffed bear. Great! Find ways to support these ideas and make them possible in the real world, not just as ideas in your head.

3. Feeling Numb

I once heard a story about the liberation of a concentration camp at the end of World War II. The American soldiers burst through the barbed wire gates, overpowering the Nazi guards. With shouts of victory, the Americans ran through the barracks, threw open the doors, freed the prisoners, and led them out to the brightness of day. Free at last!

The bone-thin prisoners poured out of the barracks, pushing and shoving, heading toward the gates. Each prisoner, upon reaching the gates, stood a few steps outside and quietly looked around. To the Americans' surprise, the prisoners did not shout for joy, did not sing or dance. No one requested a ride to town to celebrate. In fact, no one spoke at all. After blinking at the brightness of the sun, breathing in a few breaths of fresh air, each prisoner slowly and quietly stumbled back into the barracks and stretched out on his assigned cot. Silence.

When I first heard this story years ago, I didn't understand why these tortured people wouldn't dance with jubilation once their torment came to an end. But recently I have been learning the difficulty of experiencing happiness, relief, security, and love. During my years of recovery, I assumed that while the pain would be difficult to face, I could quite easily accept the good things. But like the concentration camp prisoners, I have found that joy can be as difficult as pain to accept. When someone offers me love, my initial reaction is rarely happiness. Instead, I often feel nothing at all. If feelings do surface, they are often feelings of anxiety, sadness, anger, or fear. Why would this be?

Whether our families were addicted to alcohol, physical abuse, emotional violence, sexual molestation, or neglect, many of us learned to survive by blocking out the bad feelings. Very much like those in the concentration camps, we became numb to *all* feelings because we hurt too much to feel anything at all.

The problem with numbing ourselves to the hurt is we also cut ourselves off from the joy. When we pretend we do not care about the disappointments, we find ourselves unable to celebrate the successes. When we pretend not to see the sadness, we also blind ourselves to the excitement. While our motive was understandable, trying to protect ourselves from childhood hurt, many of us chose an indirect and ineffective method of self-protection. Unknowingly, we set up ourselves to become addicts by becoming compulsively attached to a substance or a process or a relationship as a way to avoid the pain.

Perhaps the skill most needed to become an addict is the ability to become numb. The pain of our childhoods was too great and our coping skills too deficient to effectively protect ourselves and grieve our losses. Different types of addicts learn differing ways of becoming numb. For example, I learned to numb myself to my own feelings of pain by becoming overly involved in the feelings of others. Some people numb their feelings through drinking, some through drugs, others through eating, an over-investment in work, or promiscuous sex.

People commonly experience a numbness at the beginning of inner-child work. Our inner child, afraid to openly express feelings, is still hiding. If you engage in active imagination or visualization and nothing seems to happen, that's okay. Be patient. As your inner child comes to believe that you are interested, attentive, and in no particular hurry, an inner trust will develop. When your inner child feels safe, the communication will begin.

4. Being Overwhelmed by Feelings

Sandi called me in tears, "I don't know why I'm crying so hard. I just needed to talk to someone."

"What happened?" I asked, deeply concerned at how upset she sounded.

"Nothing really," she said between sobs. "I've been learning to play with my inner child and she wanted to make brownies. I thought that was great because I like brownies, so I got out the box. But as soon as I smelled the faint odor of the mix, I suddenly started to cry!"

I asked, "Do you think something happened to you when you were little, a memory prompted by the brownie mix?"

There was a long pause as she reflected. "No," Sandi said. "You know, it feels more like grief. I think I'm grieving for all the time I wanted my mom to cook with me or do special projects, but since she was so sick, she never could."

Inner-child work triggers a variety of feelings. Sometimes, like Sandi, I felt grief over the playtimes I have lost. Other times, a rush of rage fills me, or shivers of fear. Whether these feelings make sense to our adult minds or not, they have significance to our inner world. Often, if we, like Sandi, take time to examine them with a friend or therapist, or perhaps ask our inner child directly, we can come to a better understanding of our reaction.

Ways to Play with Your Inner Child

While I suspect that your inner child has plenty of ideas about fun things to do, I'll describe a variety of play activities you and your inner child may enjoy doing together. Child development experts divide play into two categories, active and passive play. Active play tends to involve physical activity and usually expends a great deal of energy. Passive play, while less physically active, can be highly creative and also can be a satisfying release of tension or expression of feelings.

1. *Dramatic Play*

Dramatic play, or make believe, is an activity that usually begins in children around the age of one and a half, peaking around the age of five. Younger children tend to use everyday scenes like playing mommy, pretending to cut the lawn like daddy, or imitating the family pet. Older children sometimes involve other children and create more complicated scenarios like playing school, pretending to be spies, or acting out parts of movies they have seen.

You may want to play dress up, pulling out old clothes stashed in the back of your closet or even going to a local thrift shop and buying some wild outfits you would never wear in public. Taking on pretend roles can help you get in touch with parts of yourself you have left behind, as well as make you giggle at your outlandish costumes.

If you have a Visual Enjoyment Style, you may want to take a picture of yourself all dressed up or pay special attention to the props you use. Your inner child probably loves playing with a variety of colors and textures. If you have a Body Enjoyment Style, what something looks like is less important than how you feel. So allow yourself to climb, run, taste, and create a convincing emotional experience. If you lean more toward an Auditory Enjoyment Style, you might want to sing folk songs you remember from childhood or pretend you are giving a speech. Whatever suits your auditory fancy.

2. Constructive Play

Children love to make things, putting various objects together to form new creations. Children up to the age of five or six tend to put objects together without a plan. As children move into latency, however, they usually create a mental image or plan prior to beginning a project. Creative activities may include making mud pies, digging tunnels in the sand, building with blocks, or stringing beads.

I have a large box in which I store a variety of building items, ready for my playtime. Whenever I spy something at the store that may contribute to my stash, I buy it for future projects. I've collected items like crayons, scissors, string, beads, clay, paint, paste, and a wide variety of colored paper. I also have some children's crafts books to give me ideas about new things I can create.

Some adults shy away from constructive play because they feel unartistic or all thumbs. Interestingly, younger children tend to be pleased with whatever they create, cheerfully displaying their creations to anyone who will stop long enough to pay attention. As we grow older, however, we become more critical of our work. Older children, if they don't feel their work compares favorably with others, may hide or even destroy their projects. As you try your hand at constructive play, I urge you to treat your inner child kindly. Relax. Who cares what your creation looks like? Take the time to praise your inner child for whatever creation results from your playtime, even if you haven't the foggiest idea what that purple thing in the drawing may be or if your clay dog looks more like a chair. After all, you are playing, not preparing for a career in art or designing the next Golden Gate bridge. This style of play is a favorite for those with a Visual Enjoyment Style.

3. Music

Music is another wonderful way to play with your inner child. Again, our adult concerns for performance may rob us of the pleasure of creating our own special brand of musical delight. Depending on the age of your inner child, you may want to explore different types of musical play. Little children like to sing, clap to music, or dance in their cribs. Once children are four or five, they are able to sing simple melodies and love to listen to music created by others.

So, pull down the shades, if you need to, and turn up the volume of your favorite record. Sing along at the top of your lungs, dancing merrily around the house. Have a great time. Who cares how you sound or if you have the right moves. You're a kid again, playing for the pleasure, not the performance.

By age seven, children may develop an interest in learning to play an instrument. As children grow older, not only do they derive pleasure from playing the instrument by themselves, but may also enjoy performing for others. Did you take piano or guitar lessons as a child? Is that flute you played in junior high school still in the garage? Why not take it out and give it a try? Others of you never had the chance to learn how to play an instrument. Now would be a great time to take up a new hobby. Your inner child would love the chance to learn to play, and it might even be fun for you as well, especially if you have an Auditory Enjoyment Style.

4. Collecting

Many children enjoy collecting a wide variety of items, not for resale or profit. There are many aspects of enjoyment to this kind of play. First, children enjoy the pleasure of acquiring their collectibles, whether through picking up shells from the beach, receiving dolls for Christmas and birthdays, or buying model airplanes. Second, collecting has a social element in that children often trade pieces of their collection, like baseball cards or marbles. Certainly the pride children receive from a prestigious collection adds a third dimension to their collecting endeavor. Lastly, children enjoy sorting, resorting, handling, and displaying their collections.

I have a collection of troll dolls I have kept from when I was a little girl that is proudly displayed in my living room, along with my stuffed animal collection. With my inner child, I have started a coin collection and a hat collection as well. There are so many things you can collect, bringing hours of enjoyment to you and your inner child, salt and pepper shakers, movie posters, Elvis memorabilia, toy cars, horse figurines. The list goes on and on. Ask your inner child what is of interest, and let the fun begin.

5. *Reading*

Reading, while physically passive, is a mentally active form of play. Younger children enjoy highly imaginative stories, usually involving animals or people engaged in fantasy stories. By the time children reach four or five, they are more interested in realistic stories like tales of adventure, love, glamour, or intrigue. Take a look around the children's book section and see what catches your eye. Are you drawn to the brightly colored books, with great illustrations but few words? Perhaps your inner child longs for you to sit and share these books together. Or maybe you are drawn to the adventure series or mystery stories. Whatever your preference, allow your inner child to pick out a book and enjoy.

Children also love to read magazines and comics. As a child, I loved comic books. The fast-moving scripts, along with the pictures, can provide hours of fun for you and your inner child. Next time you are at the store, check the comic book section. Put down that thick book analyzing the political climate of the cosmos. It's time to have some fun.

6. *Games and Sports*

Games tend to be contests of mental prowess, while sports focus on physical expertise. Both are wonderful socializing opportunities for children of all ages. Select your game with the age of your inner child in mind. You may want simple board games if your inner child is young, or more complicated card games if your inner child is older.

Certainly sports of all kinds provide a great opportunity for play. Gather some of your friends together for touch football, volleyball or miniature golf. And remember, you are playing with your inner child, so winning is not the point. Enjoy the process of play. This style of play is a favorite for those of you with the Body Enjoyment Style.

7. Movies and Television

You and your inner child may enjoy watching a wide variety of children's movies and television programs. Recently, I rented a series of videos of fairy tales such as Sleeping Beauty and Snow White. With video rental stores on nearly every corner, these enjoyable films can be seen again and again.

In many locations, vintage television shows are also now available on video. Depending on your age, you may want to reacquaint yourself with characters that were significant to you when you were a child.

8. Water Play

Another form of play is water play. Joanne Hendrick, in *The Whole Child*, writes that "water play is one of the freest, finest play opportunities we can offer children. . . . Water play is absorbing and soothing. Children will stay with it for a long time and come away refreshed and relaxed."[1]

Be honest now, don't you think it's time to get a rubber duckie for your bathroom? I'll admit it, I have one in mine, along with a few other water toys. Remember bubble baths and the fun you had playing in the tub when you were a child? Why not pick up a box of bubble bath the next time you are out and have yourself some fun during your next bath?

Other forms of water play include swimming, running through the sprinklers, playing in the waves at the beach, sliding down the rapids of a stream, and wading in a pond. Water is a wonderful way to play with your inner child.

Try Out New Ways to Play

These are just a few suggestions. No doubt, your inner child will have some more. I strongly urge you take the time to explore these avenues of play. These activities contain a genuine healing power, a power that can mend the damage you experienced as a child. But even more importantly, you must learn how to experience the joy of childhood play. Without this experience, it is nearly impossible to enjoy life.

So, do something wonderful for yourself. Give yourself the opportunity to return to those days gone by and relive, redo, renew, and replay those times in your life that didn't come out the way you wished. If you let your inner child be your guide to play, you will undoubtedly come to enjoy life in a deeper, richer, and more relaxed manner.

10

Invent New Ways to Enjoy Life as an Adult

Are you having fun yet?

Many of us have distorted views of fun, confusing fun with our addictions. To some, fun has meant drinking all night, then stumbling home in the wee hours of the morning. To others, fun was having sex with forbidden partners. If you can believe it, I used to think it was fun to work seven days a week helping others. (I think we codependents are the least able to have fun. We didn't even choose an exciting addiction!)

Have you allowed yourself to explore your passions? Do you know what gives you pleasure, nourishment, and that "wow-isn't-it-great-to-be-alive" feeling?

Six years ago, my Potential Pleasures List looked like this:

1. Work full-time in the field of child abuse prevention, then volunteer an extra twenty hours at my church.
2. Serve on as many committees as will take me, volunteer to take the minutes, type up the reports, and make copies for all committee members.
3. Make the most of my free time by watching movies on

current social issues like divorce, child abuse, poverty, and discrimination so that I will be inspired to do more good works.

4. Become romantically involved with men who depend on me to sort out their problems and who make me feel needed.

Phew! I sure knew how to have a good time, didn't I? Well, now my Potential Pleasures List looks more like this:

1. Share my journey in a creative way through writing and speaking, at a pace that feels natural.
2. Enjoy High Tea in the afternoon with a friend.
3. Watch movies that make me laugh and are entertaining.
4. Share the beauty of a sunset with the man I love while saying nothing at all.

What is on your Potential Pleasures List? Take the effort to write out a list of activities and experiences that nurture you. Knowing your personal Enjoyment Style will greatly assist you in generating new and nurturing ideas for play and passion. Another helpful tool is identifying whether you are best replenished and nurtured through introverted or extroverted activities.

Introverts and Extroverts

I used to feel sorry for introverts, seeing them as shy, socially inept creatures who kept to themselves and lived lonely, pathetic lives. In contrast, I considered myself to be an extroverted, socially adept, attractive person with many friends. After taking a more honest look at myself and clearing up my misconceptions about the true nature of introversion and extroversion, I surprisingly discovered I was an introvert.

The terms *introvert* and *extrovert* do not describe whether a person has the ability to interact with others. Those social skills can be learned by anyone of any temperament. Extroverts care about the external world and are energized by being related to what is going on around them and outside of themselves. Introverts care about the inner world of ideas and feelings. In contrast to extroverts, introverts are energized by what goes on inside themselves and those factors that influence and change their inner world. Extroverts often want to talk about what they are doing in the world, and introverts often want to talk about what they are feeling or thinking.

Consider introversion and extroversion as ends of a continuum. The pure introvert delights in solitude and often finds nurturance in exterior stillness and creative interaction with his or her own thoughts and feelings. This is the interior landscape of discovery and significance for the introvert. The introvert cares little about external events or activities, even to the point of neglect or indifference unless a major conflict arises.

The pure extrovert, at the other extreme, is enlivened by external activity and does not want to miss out on the action. He or she is not really concerned about what is going on in the interior unless it causes a serious emotional or intellectual conflict.

Most of us fall somewhere in between these two extremes, and may move back and forth along the continuum, even though our individual temperament and personality will usually be biased toward one end or the other all through life. On some days a party energizes me, but on other days I adore time all to myself. Sometimes I am nurtured through talking with one special friend, and other times I prefer a larger gathering.

Where do you fall on the introversion-extroversion continuum? If you could do anything you wanted, what would you like to do? Run away to a quiet beach to be alone with your inner feelings? Or dance the night away in a boisterous crowd?

There is no right way or wrong way to receive nurturance. However, we must all identify who we really are and what is most important to us, what we really care about. This is difficult in a society that is extroverted and values action and external activity far more than it does interior reflection. Finding ways to play that are meaningful for you takes courage, especially if they don't fit the normal expectations of other people.

Invent New Ways to Play

You are now armed with vital information about yourself. You have identified your personal Enjoyment Style, recovered your childlike enjoyment of play, and discovered where you fall on the introversion-extroversion continuum. With this information in mind, you can create a variety of activities and experiences that are, dare I say, fun. Some of your ideas probably can be enjoyed alone while others probably include one or more of your friends. Here are some of my ideas.

Visual Enjoyment Style
- Spend the afternoon at an art museum.
- Attend a foreign movie festival, selecting the films with scenic shots of exotic lands.
- Take a photography class, cultivating your special enjoyment of sight.
- Take an elevator ride to the top of the highest building in your city and enjoy the view.
- Buy a set of watercolors and paint a picture.
- Keep a set of art or picture books in your office or home so when you have a few minutes during the day you can nurture your soul by delighting your vision.
- Watch an exciting basketball, baseball, or football game.
- Look in the mirror and give yourself your very best smile.
- Imagine that you are seeing your Higher Power, who is giving you a gift.

Body Enjoyment Style
- Spend the afternoon at a skating rink enjoying the sheer pleasure of movement.
- Treat yourself to your favorite flavor of ice cream.
- Take ballroom dance lessons.

- Buy a soft sweater or flannel shirt and wear it just because it feels good.
- Go to the beach and play in the sand.
- Join a local volleyball team.
- Get a professional massage.
- Give yourself a hug.
- Dance your feelings of appreciation for the love you have received from God.

Auditory Enjoyment Style
- Gather together some friends and sing folk songs.
- Unplug the phone and enjoy the silence.
- Spend an evening at a local club listening to jazz.
- Buy a CD of your favorite music.
- Attend a poetry reading.
- Enjoy an intimate conversation with a special friend.
- Learn to play an instrument.
- Treat yourself to a night at a local comedy club.
- Tell yourself aloud, "I love you."
- Sing a song of praise to your Higher Power.

Combining Enjoyment Styles

Even though I primarily have an Auditory Enjoyment Style, I also receive a great deal of pleasure through the other two channels. The fact that we enjoy one style more than the others doesn't mean we can't open ourselves to pleasures the other styles may provide. Often, I combine styles to create wonderful experiences. Here are some suggestions for what I call combination fun.

- Sun by the pool while sipping a delicious fruit drink (body), and talking with a group of friends (auditory).
- Hike up a mountain trail (body) while listening to classical music on your Walkman (auditory) and then admire a glorious view once you reach the summit (visual).
- Enjoy the silence (auditory) and the splendor of the snow

(visual) while cross-country skiing (body) with a close friend.

- Watch an action-adventure movie (visual and auditory).
- Dance cheek-to-cheek (body) while your favorite romantic music plays (auditory).
- Cook a great meal (body), set a beautiful table with candles and flowers (visual), put on soft music (auditory) and invite someone you love to join you for dinner.
- Receive a professional massage (body) while listening to instrumental music (auditory) and visualizing beautiful landscapes (visual).

What are the special combinations you can create for yourself? What have you always wanted to do, but never have given yourself permission to explore? What have you kept yourself from experiencing because of a past belief in scarcity? Now that you know that any positive experience can and should be yours, what would you like to do? How can you best delight yourself through your sense of sight? Touch? Smell? Hearing? Taste? How can you nurture yourself intellectually? Physically? Emotionally? Spiritually? Give yourself permission to play, explore, and investigate. There is enough, so you have no reason to hold yourself back. Don't limit your list because an idea may seem too outlandish or unaffordable. Allow your imagination free rein. Create the most passionate, exciting Potential Pleasures List you can imagine.

11

Share the Celebration

In the last chapter, we developed a list of wonderful activities we could do by ourselves or with others. Creating that list was important, but having a piece of paper with some fun ideas written on it won't increase the abundance and passion in your life. Developing an Effective Enjoyment Strategy is worthless if you do not implement it. Take the next step in this process. Abandon yourself to the passion of play.

Shame and Scarcity Questions

I visited Anna, a friend whose son, Jason, had just turned two. Anna greeted me and welcomed me into her home. Screeching with delight, Jason dashed into the hallway heading toward the den, unaware of my arrival and quite enthralled with his toy. Suddenly, he stopped, dropped to the floor, and wiggled out of his training pants. Completely naked, he continued his gleeful romp into the den.

Anna tilted her head and gave me a long, tired smile. "I can't keep clothes on that child," she moaned. "He loves to run around the house naked."

I thought of Adam and Eve enjoying the delights of the Garden of Eden: "And they were both naked, the man and his wife, and were not ashamed" (Gen. 2:25). Like our ancestors who were once free of shame, Jason had yet to feel self-conscious about his body. Unaware of the social taboos and restrictions, the child was still free to enjoy himself in a most natural way.

Unlike Jason, we in recovery have learned many lessons about shame. We were raised in a dysfunctional society that promotes a Perspective of Scarcity. Shame is a major outgrowth of this perspective. We were made to feel ashamed of our legitimate needs, ashamed of our wishes and desires, ashamed of our bodies and our passions. Fearing the shame of appearing selfish, we tried to hide our true selves. This shame undermines our self-esteem and our ability to enjoy life. Unashamed, Jason was alive to the playful pleasures available in this world. Central to recovering the art of play is the recovery from the shame that keeps us fearful of celebration.

In an earlier chapter we discussed the importance of taking responsibility for our own happiness. When we don't take responsibility for our own enjoyment, we wait passively for others to take care of us. Rarely does this work to our advantage.

Some of us, however, err on the other end of the continuum. We have given up hope that anyone will care for us or nurture us. Usually the childhood victim of neglect or abandonment, this inner child mutters scarcity questions like "What's the use of asking for anything? Who would help me anyway?" At the suggestion that your potential pleasure list could be shared with someone else, you may hear an inner voice ask, "What? Are you crazy? Show someone this list and risk being laughed at?" Urging you to invite someone over to enjoy a special activity may conjure up an incredulous, "What if I ask someone to come over and they say no? How could I stand the rejection? How could I bear to see them again when I'd feel so embarrassed?"

There is a well-worn, often-used strategy promoted by

those entrenched in shame. It's called "Why don't we wish really hard and hope that someone will read our minds?"

I once saw a magic show where a woman went into the audience and touched the hand of a person in the audience. A man sitting on the stage, dressed in a tuxedo, claimed to have the power to read people's minds. Without having any previous information, this man rattled off birth dates and wedding anniversaries, names of siblings, and described events impossible to guess. The show was great.

I do not have a clue as to how the trick worked, but I can assure you that what makes for a great magic act does not work in day-to-day relationships. Directed by the magical thinking of a wounded inner child, we find ourselves hiding our Potential Pleasures List, expecting our friends to somehow know what we want or need. The only way we can receive what we need is to ask for it.

Take the Risk and Ask for What You Need

Those of us who wait for others to read our minds rarely have a good time. I urge you to embrace the Perspective of Abundance by reframing the questions you ask yourself. Instead of assuming that others magically know what you need and are purposefully depriving you, ask, "What are the ways I can communicate what I would like? How can I ask, clearly and directly, for the things I need?"

Does this mean that every time you ask for what you need, you will get it? Unfortunately not. Sometimes when we ask, we get "no" for an answer. The risk of rejection can be so frightening that we simply refuse to reveal our needs.

As you take responsibility for your own happiness, you will develop a variety of activities and a network of people who are nurturing to you. This support system creates a broad based support that decreases the loss due to a "no" from any one person. When I have three friends who might be interested in going out with me, finding that the first person I ask is busy does not leave me alone and feeling dejected. I still have two more people on my list, and chances are one of them will be available. The more nurturance you cultivate for yourself, the less dependent you become on any one person or activity. As a consequence, those around you may find you less demanding and more inviting, more attractive and easier to nurture.

The anxiety associated with potential rejection can be decreased if you apply what you learned about discerning your Enjoyment Style to your friends and family. When you contemplate who you want to invite to join you for an activity, think about that person's Enjoyment Style. By matching a person's Enjoyment Style with a particular activity beforehand, you increase the likelihood that your invitation will be accepted because that person will likely share your passion for the activity.

If you are in the mood for little conversation but a lot of activity, avoid inviting your friend with an Introverted Auditory Enjoyment Style. Find someone with an Extroverted Body Enjoyment Style to match your mood. Conversely, if you want to drive to the hills and see the lights, skip over your friend with an Extroverted Body Enjoyment Style and call one with a Visual Enjoyment Style who falls somewhere near the middle of the introvert-extrovert spectrum.

Of course, you may have special people in your life with different Enjoyment Strategies with whom you want to share a great many experiences. Again, understanding differing Enjoyment Strategies can aid in negotiating more pleasurable experiences. Since we live in a world of abundance, no one has to go without what he or she needs. By sharing a Perspective of Abundance, you can work together to create experiences that are mutually satisfying and increase your love and intimacy.

Inviting Others to Share the Passion of Play

One morning recently, I was working out to a new aerobics video in my living room. Puffing along and enjoying myself, I followed the video instructor through a wide variety of movements, when suddenly I burst into tears. Completely taken off guard, I sobbed intensely for several minutes, but continued dancing to the video. After I'd finished my workout and my tears had subsided, I replayed the tape at the spot that had triggered my outburst.

The movement was a joyous dance step where the arms are extended wide and the chest exposed. The instructor said joyfully, "Celebrate! Use this movement to tell the world, 'Hey, here I am!'"

As I reviewed the tape, I realized that my tears had been a release of shame-based feelings. Celebrating myself is hard to do. Opening up myself in the physical expression of that particular dance step, even in the safety of my own living room, triggered fear and anxiety. Showing others that I am having a good time and feel good about myself can be an extremely threatening thing to do.

Most of us are comfortable with the thought of a child asking another child, "Will you come out and play with me?" However, as adults, turning to another adult and asking him or her to play with us may be considered inappropriate, or even an invitation for sexual involvement. We may associate playing with other adults with sex because we know, unconsciously, that the passion in the art of playing is very, very powerful.

When we play, we enjoy ourselves, we celebrate ourselves. Those of us from dysfunctional backgrounds have been taught to be ashamed of ourselves and may be reluctant to be vulnerable during the passion of play. We must trust another person before we are able to relax to the point of genuinely enjoying ourselves or abandoning ourselves to the moment.

As a consultant, writer, and speaker, I work with a large number of talented and often intense people. Without noticing, we can become singularly focused on a project, excitedly sharing our creativity. I now make it a practice to suggest, after a particularly intense session, we go out, relax, and have some fun. I have received a variety of reactions to this suggestion, anything from, "Sure, that sounds great. We deserve some downtime after all this work," to stunned silences and looks of terror.

When we have fun with another person, when we share the passion of play, we naturally and spontaneously develop intimacy. The less self-conscious we are about our enjoyment the more childlike we become. We release our inner child to express genuine delight and enjoyment. We naturally discard our shame for the sheer pleasure of the moment. As a result, we experience a powerful passion for living.

We spontaneously feel thrilled to be alive, and we associate that joyous sensation with those who have shared the moment. Many of us fear incorporating play into our lives because we unconsciously know that when we share play's passion with another person, we are sharing a particular form of love. Sadly, we unconsciously resist play because we also unconsciously resist intimacy. We deprive ourselves by placing play and intimacy outside of our Enjoyment Comfort Zone.

As outlined previously, you must recognize these unconscious saboteurs throughout this journey toward enjoyment. Uncover those misassociations. Properly place positive experiences within your Enjoyment Comfort Zone and remove any attractions to destructive experiences. Step by step, you can learn to trust yourself and others to safely enjoy the passion of play. And as you cultivate the art of play, you will find that you are also cultivating your capacity to love.

12

Notice the Nurturance Available

Having fun is not as easy as it looks. Learning to enjoy life, to receive the nourishment available, is a difficult task. Many of us have had to revamp our personal paradigms, redefining how we look at life in general. Quite a major undertaking.

As you review your Potential Pleasures List, you might be asking yourself, "Can I really have all these things? Isn't this just a wish list? How could I possibly afford a weekly massage, a trip to Hawaii, a new stereo system, or tuition for the classes I want? I can barely get by on the money I have now. How can I possibly pay for all of this so-called abundance she keeps talking about? And what about the guilt I'd feel spending all this time and money on myself? Ugh! I feel guilty just thinking about it."

Ah, there are those scarcity questions, again.

Did you think learning how to play would be easy? Well, it's not. If you decide to bring the passion of play into your recovery, it will redefine your relationships. If you insist on receiving your share, your life will be changed. Nothing less is required. If you trade a Perspective of Scarcity for a Perspective of Abundance, you will transform your life.

If having fun were easy, we'd all be doing it already. Unfortunately, we have been so damaged, so fundamentally trained to endure abuse and deprivation, that our lives have to change radically if we are to embrace a genuine passion for living and cultivate the art of play. We will need to discard our well-honed deprivation skills.

Discarding Our Deprivation Skills

Deprivation skills, grounded in a Perspective of Scarcity, are developed as a dysfunctional way of protecting ourselves from the pain of disappointment and the shame of rejection. I am quite adept at deprivation skills, and I have observed others whom I would consider qualified to teach graduate courses in the subject.

We learn to tolerate deprivation, or even endure abuse, rather than insist our needs be addressed. For example, assuming we can't have access to the financial resources available, we may refrain from asking for a raise or from interviewing for a better paying job. Instead, we focus our attention on ways we can cut back on our expenses. While I am not promoting irresponsible or erratic spending patterns, I do believe that many of us, mired in a Perspective of Scarcity, are unconsciously motivated to use our creativity to develop ways of depriving ourselves of life's enjoyment rather than apply our energy to enlarging our enjoyment comfort zones.

We ask ourselves scarcity questions such as, "How can I cut back this month?" "What are the luxuries I don't absolutely need?" "How am I wasting money?" and "What can I do without?"

We deprive ourselves of the flowers we want to decorate the dining room table, sit at home while our friends attend the theater, or postpone having our hair cut even though we can hardly see through our bangs. We prefer to suffer deprivation rather than invest our energy in getting our needs met.

If we took the risk of adopting the Perspective of Abundance, we could ask ourselves, "Which items on my Potential Pleasures List do I want to enjoy this month?" "How much money will these experiences cost me?" and "How can I apply my creativity to obtaining the money I need?"

Deprivation skills are not limited to finances. Many of us are so accustomed to depriving ourselves that we do so even when money is not the constraining factor. In fact, sometimes our deprivation skills actually cost us more money. For example, we fear appearing selfish when having dinner with friends, so we insist on paying for the entire check. The next night we have to stay home because we already spent our weekend entertainment allowance.

We pay for our deprivation skills in other ways as well, through our health, energy, and time. I travel a great deal in my work, and for years I was unwilling to have a porter carry my bags because I didn't want to waste the money. After all, I could carry them myself. I am learning that a two-dollar tip is actually less expensive to me than the monetary value I put on doctor's bills due to physical exertion, bruises on my legs, and sore back muscles.

When we are sick and our friends offer to bring us groceries, those of us adept in deprivation skills will instinctively say, "Oh, no thanks." We will drag ourselves to the store, sick and pathetic, perhaps prolonging our illness and costing us more days from work. Or, perhaps you are the kind who goes to work, sick or not, intent on depriving yourself of the rest you need.

Remember that nothing is free. Nothing. If we don't pay for it with money, we will pay for it with our time, energy, or health. We may ride the bus instead of taking a plane and save some of the fare, but we will lose more than what we saved through the expenditure of the additional travel time and back aches. We delude ourselves when we believe that our deprivation skills are cost-effective.

When you deprive yourself of what you need, you are not saving yourself, you are wasting yourself. You deplete your emotional reserve. You tax your physical energy. You may even decrease the length of your life. Deprivation skills are rooted in the position of scarcity and are addictive in nature. Like all addictive processes, a lifestyle of deprivation can lead to premature death.

Naming Your Needs

It is critical that you discard your deprivation skills and implement instead your enjoyment strategy. Naming your needs and insisting on enough will result in a powerful change in your life. I urge you to review your Potential Pleasures List and begin asking yourself abundance questions: "Which one of these can I enjoy immediately?" "How can I incorporate these activities into my life on a regular basis?" "Who would like to join me in this endeavor?" "How can I open up myself to God's nurturance in a deeper way?" "How can I more fully embrace a passion for living?" "What nurturance do God and others offer me that I am overlooking?"

Notice the Nurturance Available

Several months ago I cleaned out my garage and found a box of letters I had kept from high school and college. As I recalled those years in my life, I remembered a host of friends, but also remembered feeling rather deprived romantically. With this rather bittersweet memory in mind, I decided to sort through the letters to select the ones I wanted to keep.

To my utter amazement, I discovered a host of love letters, from quite a few men. One of these relationships was with a man who lived out of state. I recalled being passionately infatuated with him but after receiving one or two letters, I believed he was not interested. But as I sorted through the box of letters, I found that I had received nearly twenty rather juicy love letters from him, full of adolescent vows of passion and cries of agony at my breaking up with him. I didn't remember it that way.

One man from Michigan wrote me for three years. Even after rereading his letters I can't remember who this man was. I have erased him from my memory altogether.

One letter from a man I do remember dating described how he had spent the evening consoling another friend of his, a man I had apparently just broken up with. They were supporting each other in their shared sorrow over being mistreated by me. While I recall spending some time with both of these men, I was unaware that either of them had any substantial romantic feelings for me or that I had in any way hurt them.

As I found many more letters from other men I thought to myself, "These must be from someone else's adolescence." I do not remember receiving these letters, nor did I receive any of the joy, affection, or affirmation such attention should bring a young woman. I also hurt people unintentionally because I missed cues. I could have enjoyed so much more than I had been able to experience.

As a therapist, I have worked with many people who have repressed traumatic memories, horrible experiences that their conscious minds were unable to contain. I was surprised to find that I had repressed not trauma but delight, not rejection but invitations to love. And, I am afraid, I am not the only person who does this. When we view life from a Perspective of Scarcity all we are able to see is deprivation, even in the face of abundance.

Are you noticing the nurturance available to you? What nurturance is being offered to you this very moment that you are overlooking? Who is trying to love you that, without a second thought, you are brushing away? Have you decided that you will only receive affection from one particular person and, therefore, discount or reject all other offers of love?

What joyful and nurturing experiences are available to you right now, perhaps in your own front yard? Do flowers grow in front of your office that you could visually enjoy? Have you opened your ears to enjoy the laughter of the children playing in the school yard across the street? Have you slowed down long enough to really savor that juicy piece of fruit you have for an afternoon snack? Are you really noticing the nurturance available?

The God of this world is a God of abundance. When we forget that we are fundamentally dependent on a Higher Power for our sanity, we can fall back into our addiction. We then can become abusive to others, taking more than our share, or abusive to ourselves, depriving ourselves of what we genuinely need. While not condoning those who hoard or take more than their share, I believe we are all entitled to our portion.

Incorporating the passion of play into our recovery begins and ends in a healthy, accurate, and positive relationship with God, the God of abundance, the God who loves us. I leave you with one of my favorite passages in scripture, a prayer from the book of Proverbs:

> Two things I asked of Thee,
> Do not refuse me before I die:
> Keep deception and lies far from me,
> Give me neither poverty nor riches;
> Feed me with the food that is my portion,
> Lest I be full and deny Thee and say, "Who is the LORD?"
> Or lest I be in want and steal,
> And profane the name of my God.
>
> (Prov. 30: 7–9)[1]

Notes

1. Rekindle Your Hope in the Possibility of Play.

1. M. Scott Peck, *The Road Less Traveled* (New York: Simon & Schuster, 1978), 44.

2. Stephen R. Covey, *The Seven Habits of Highly Effective People* (New York: Simon & Schuster, 1989), 23.

3. Thomas S. Kuhn, *The Structure of Scientific Revolutions* (Chicago: Univ. of Chicago Press, 1970), 23.

4. Peck, 46.

2. Embrace the Perspective of Abundance.

1. Peck, 105.

3. Enlarge the Limits of Your Enjoyment Comfort Zone.

1. Robert K. Johnston, *The Christian at Play* (Grand Rapids: Eerdmans, 1983), 4.

2. Wayne E. Oates, *Confessions of a Workaholic* (Nashville: Abingdon Press, 1971), 12.

3. Walter Kerr, *The Decline of Pleasure* (New York: Simon & Schuster, 1962), 48.

4. Acknowledge the Value of Play.

1. Joanne Hendrick, *The Whole Child* (St. Louis: C.V. Mosby, 1975), 169.

2. Hendrick, 171.

3. Claudia Black, *It Will Never Happen to Me: Children of*

Alcoholics as Youngsters-Adolescents-Adults (New York: Ballantine, 1981), 24–28.

5. Open Yourself to Your Inner Child.
   1. John Bradshaw, *Home Coming: Reclaiming & Championing Your Inner Child* (New York: Bantam Books, 1990), 57.
   2. Bradshaw, 57.
   3. Robert A. Johnson, *Inner Work: Using Dreams & Active Imagination for Personal Growth* (San Francisco: Harper, 1986), 138.

6. Insist on Safety for You and Your Inner Child.
   1. Peck, 105.

7. Accept Responsibility for Your Own Enjoyment.
   1. Susan Jeffers, *Opening Our Hearts to Men* (New York: Fawcett, 1989), 27.
   2. Lewis B. Smedes, *Forgive & Forget: Healing the Hurts We Don't Deserve* (San Francisco: Harper, 1984), 29.
   3. Ellen Bass and Laura Davis, *The Courage to Heal: A Guide for Women Survivors of Child Sexual Abuse* (New York: HarperCollins, 1988), 150.

9. Explore New Ways to Play with Your Inner Child.
   1. Hendrick, 95.

12. Notice the Nurturance Available.
   1. THE NEW AMERICAN STANDARD BIBLE, Copyright © 1960, 1962, 1963, 1968, 1971, 1972, 1973, 1975, 1977 by The Lockman Foundation. Used by permission.

About the Author

Carmen Renee Berry is a noted lecturer, author, and workshop and retreat leader. With over ten years of experience in the area of child sexual abuse prevention and treatment, Carmen specializes in overcoming childhood trauma, burnout prevention, integration of spirituality and recovery, and the use of bodywork in the recovery process. Carmen holds two masters degrees in social sciences and social work and is certified by the State of California as a massage techician. She is a co-founder of the National Association for Christian Recovery and writes a regular column in *STEPS* entitled "Surviving and Thriving." Currently Carmen serves as a senior staff member for The Recovery Partnership, the sponsor of the National Association for Christian Recovery. She can be contacted through:

The Recovery Partnership
P.O. Box 11095
Whittier, California 90603
310/697-6201